LIVINGtouch

INtouch

WOMEN OF FAITH IN THE 90s

Marsha Spradlin

New Hope
Birmingham, Alabama

New Hope
P. O. Box 12065
Birmingham, AL 35202-2065

Dewey Decimal Classification: 248.843
Subject Headings: CHRISTIAN LIFE—WOMEN
                  WOMEN—SOCIAL CONDITIONS
                  WOMEN—UNITED STATES
   Scripture quotations marked NIV are from the Holy Bible, New Inter-
national Version. Copyright © 1973, 1977, 1984 International Bible Society.
Used by permission of Zondervan Bible Publishers.
   Scripture quotations marked TLB are from The Living Bible, copyright 1971
by Tyndale House Publishers, Wheaton, IL. Used by permission.
   Scripture quotations marked KJV are from The Holy Bible, King James
Version.
   Scripture quotation marked NASB is from the New American Standard
Bible, © The Lockman Foundation 1960, 1962, 1963, 1968, 1971, 1972, 1973,
1975, 1977. Used by permission.

Thanks to the Home Mission Board of the Southern Baptist Convention for
many of the statistics found in this book.

Cover design by Janell Young

N904106 • 10M • 0690

ISBN: 0-936625-89-9

To
Pat Ritchie
and
Sara Ann Hobbs

Your lives have strengthened the faith of all who know
and love you.

Special thanks to
my editor and friend
Cathy Butler

and to the many women of faith whose stories are tucked
between these pages.

Contents

Author's note
The stories told are based on true life experiences. Because of their sensitive nature, the names, locations, and personalities may be a composite. This in no way distorts my perception of the truth; for long before this book was written, it was lived by hundreds of women—any one of whom could be you or me.

Introduction

. . . We are homemakers,
> community leaders,
> teachers,
> students,
> volunteers,
> nurses,
> accountants,
> and more.

. . . We are ordinary women
> who believe in and serve
> an extraordinary God.

. . . We have families to care for,
> church responsibilities to fulfill,
> careers to pursue,
> relationships to develop,
> classes to attend,
> and volunteer work to carry out.

Balancing the many dimensions of our lives often is not easy, but we must if we are to establish right priorities. And the priorities we establish today can make a big difference in our world and our children's world tomorrow.

Regardless of age, vocation, or education, women of faith in the 1990s share a common goal: to represent our extraordinary Lord in an extraordinary time. Those of us who are born into the family of God through faith in Jesus Christ not only have the privilege of being God's daughters but also His representatives. Our mission could be defined sim-

1

ply as telling about Jesus in a day when women are confronted with so many choices that we feel immobilized.

How do we choose to be His representatives in our quick-fix, fast-lane society where life seems frantic and out of control? When do we find time to touch the life of another in an age that seems to be traveling faster than the speed of light?

Managing our lives has become not unlike a juggling act in which we are forced to drop one ball of responsibility in order to pick up another. Most aspects of our lives are in constant motion; we are literally moving targets.

We are women of the 1990s. Never has a generation of women had so many options and opportunities. But tightly woven with our opportunities and options is oppression. As women move from the labor room to the boardroom, and vice versa, we struggle for clarity and commitment. Yet our opportunities seem paradoxical as they embrace both independence and dependence. As we obtain education and move into the labor force, we delay marriage and child-bearing, thus acquiring independence. Yet for many women their newly owned independence creates a backlash of dependence. Women have others depending on them in new ways. For example:

- Fifty percent of the adult female population heads a household.
- Over half of all children under age 18 have mothers in the labor force.
- Half of all married women with children under age 6 work outside of the home.
- Women hold two out of three of all jobs paying minimum wage.
- Eight of ten of the poor are women with children.

Obviously, the thrill of newly acquired independence may be offset by the pressures and confusion of our newly created dependence. As a result, women of the 1990s lead depleted lives. Both positive and negative pressures force women to look for guidance from those women whose paths preceded their own. But women of the 1990s often find only a gaping abyss instead of a path. We have few role models.

We are women in motion. Our hectic, pressured, competitive lives have led us down a road called exhaustion. Too often our lives are already so crowded that there is little room for anything or anyone else.

If we are to be authentic representatives of the Father's kingdom, if we wish to be perceived by today's woman as relevant, we must address the challenges distinctive to women, young and old, in the 1990s. To address these challenges, we must ask ourselves

- Can we effectively reach all of today's women for Christ without giving up our traditional approaches?
- Can diversity and unity coexist?
- Have achievement and success delivered the personal fulfillment that many have sought?

These are difficult questions to ask and answer. It would be far easier to ignore the oppression and crises facing women and concentrate only on our newly acquired opportunities. To find the answers, we must use our most innovative thinking, thinking that is empowered by our Lord. Innovative thinking is also a paradox: it is all-inspiring, yet painful as we are asked to lay aside, for the moment, all preconceptions of who we are as Christian women.

For these reasons, I have found this book difficult to research and equally difficult to write. But if we are to come INtouch with ourselves; our roles; our relationships to our families, co-workers, and our Father, these issues cannot be ignored.

Hope still prevails in the brief space between our many commitments. Could it be that our quest for this meaning has surfaced because we now recognize that our visible achievements do not satisfy our deepest desires? If so, we continue to search for fulfillment.

For many the search for continuity and meaning is now

drawing women of the 1990s into the spiritual arena, where cults flourish.

As believers, we know that only Jesus can fill the void in our lives. As we are INtouch with a variety of women every day—mothers in car pools, co-workers at coffee break, or students sharing a dormitory room—we may ask, How can I get to know her in such a way that I could share Jesus Christ with her?[1]

Perhaps the only way to touch the lives of those women near you is to develop a relevant relationship. But, to touch a life, you must first be INtouch with our Father and then yourself. Only then will you be INtouch with who "they" are and how "they" think.

As we struggle for identity, clarity, and commitment, there is One to Whom we can look for direction. As Jesus' INtouch ministry unfolded, the average citizen of Israel observed His extraordinary approach to women, one that cut against the grain of commonly held practices. Jesus was INtouch with their pain.

"Jesus treated women as no man had ever treated them before. His warmth, personal attention, tenderness, sound teaching, and compassion toward women was revolutionary. He openly demonstrated His love for each individual He met—both men and women—for whom He would ultimately die."[2]

Two thousand years have passed. As women of a high-tech society begin to turn their attention toward the future, we find that we do have something in common with all women who have gone before us. The quest for fulfillment has been, and perhaps shall always be, the driving force which urges us to press on, to excel, and to reach those things that our mothers and grandmothers could not attain; though, perhaps, they dreamed of such attainments. Because of this drive, women are in top leadership positions in corporate boardrooms, sports arenas, and academic life.[3]

As we become INtouch with women living in our world, we are confronted with a diversity of needs, needs not like those of our mothers or grandmothers. Diverse needs confronting today's woman include poverty, divorce, domestic violence, balancing children and careers, emotional distress, chemical dependence, the time crunch, the three-generation family, and restlessness. How do we, women of faith, reach out and touch the lives of the hurting women in our world?

INtouch (Women of Faith in the 90s) is a book about women, ordinary women who have recognized that they serve an extraordinary God.

In each chapter I will tell you about two types of women: women experiencing social, moral, domestic, and even career crisis; and women of faith who are following Jesus' example by nurturing and affecting change in their lives.

As you read, keep in mind that each story is based on true life experience. As you gain valuable insights into the lives of women of our generation, I pray you will be motivated by the numerous stories of ordinary women who share their time, love, and commitment in order to make a difference in someone's life; women who are living out their faith in this highly mobile, fast-paced society.

We must realize there are still many problems. A section in each chapter called "Getting INtouch" will raise your awareness level regarding many social and moral problems and trends affecting today's woman.

But we cannot stop there. The ball is in your court the moment your eyes arrive at the section entitled "Getting Involved." This is your opportunity to put your best thinking to work. Continue to imagine that we are sitting together. This time you are doing the talking as you share with me your ideas of ways to touch the life of someone you know.

It is my sincere prayer that you capture insights that will encourage you to take the risk to reach out in His name. As we touch the lives of others in Jesus' name, we are likewise touched by the One Whose love breaks down all barriers. As we realize our responsibility, may we embrace the sisterhood of all women with renewed sensitivity.

---

[1]Helen Ashker, *Jesus Cares for Women* (Colorado Springs, CO: NavPress, 1987), 12.

[2]Ibid., 16.

[3]Ibid., 12.

PART I

ACROSS GENERATIONS

1

Crossing Generations

Your kingdom is an everlasting kingdom, and your dominion
endures through all generations.

Psalm 145:13 (NIV)

Her voice was meek, gentle, and worn. Even though I
tried desperately to cling to her every word, my thoughts
escaped. Imagine being born in 1909 and joining the ranks
of working women at age nine.

I couldn't avoid being captivated by what seemed to ex-
emplify a well-written novel, for her life's experiences told
a colorful story. I sought to capture each brilliant detail of
what would become a portrait of words—words filled with
energy and imagination. I continued to listen.

"Mama, Papa, my seven sisters and three brothers, and
I settled in Danielsville, Georgia. Since I was the second
oldest girl at home, I quit attending my one-room school
the day after my ninth birthday. After all, Mama needed
another pair of hands in the kitchen.

"My chores started at daylight. There was no alarm clock.
Back then you got up usually because you were cold. For
me, cooking was the hardest. My hands were still so tiny.
But my hands soon grew strong. Kneading dough and carrying heavy wood and pork sides from the smokehouse has
a way of building little girls into strong women.

"At times I got so tired I wanted to cry. But I couldn't
cry, not in front of Mama. After all, she had enough worries.
Crippling arthritis kept her in bed most of the time. But at

9

least she was well enough to help by telling me what to do. Since Mama was sick, my sister Bell helped me take care of the babies.

"Breakfast was always the same: pork, eggs, coffee, and gravy; all cooked on the wood stove. Breakfast was hardly over before it was time to start lunch. Having to wash dishes with well-drawn water took time. Lunch, like breakfast, seldom varied. We had corn bread and milk, and always fresh apple cobbler. What was left over was usually saved for dinner. But with that many mouths to feed, well, I almost always had to start dinner from scratch too. That meant milking our two cows and gathering sweet potatoes.

"Except for breakfast, meat was scarce. Not only could we not afford meat, we had nowhere to store it. Those were the days before iceboxes. Our wood-burning stove didn't have a hot closet (a hot closet was a place to keep food fresh). We could keep milk, though. My younger sister and I would pour leftover milk in fruit jars and carefully lower it into the well. I'll never forget the taste—icy cold!"

"What did you do for fun?" I quickly asked. "After all, you were still a little girl."

"Fun, oh, fun wasn't what it is today. Except for the babies, we all had jobs. It took all of us working from sunrise to bedtime to get the chores done. After working 14 hours a day, we were exhausted. Because work took up so much of our day, we tried to make our work fun. My brothers worked the fields with Papa while my sisters and I did the household chores.

"Bell's job was ironing. I felt sorry for Bell. Our five-pound iron had to be heated on the wood stove several times to iron just one of Papa's shirts. We didn't have an ironing board. But a board on top of two straight-back chairs worked just fine. Fun . . . we made work fun. We talked and told stories. Our imagination was our only limitation.

"At Christmas we did get a toy; that is, if Papa had work in the coal mines. I remember one Christmas. It was the best one in all of my 82 years. Bell and I got a little China doll. I bet I imagined making a hundred trips to China with that little doll.

"Because Bell and I were the oldest girls we did all the shopping for our family of 13, Mama and Papa included. It seemed like a long trip to Comer. The trip to Comer and back took all day, even though it was only 15 miles. I used to wish that Danielsville had as many merchants as Comer.

"I was only 11 when Mama and Papa divorced. Nowadays divorce seems popular. Well, it was popular then too. We moved to Grandpa's house in Alabama. After Papa left, my work really began. But we pulled together more than ever.

"Every day seemed the same, at least until I turned 19. It was that year that I thought my whole world would change. Change for me came in a tall, handsome, and witty package. His eyes were steel blue. We courted in an old buggy until we were married in 1928. Nineteen may seem young, but being a single girl then was rare.

"I was ill prepared for the years that followed. I thought life had been hard before. But one year after I married Ira, I learned what hard was.

"My husband lost his job at the railroad because of the depression. Like other men, he was forced to do the only thing he was trained to do—he farmed. Ira bought a cow and mule on credit. In fact, everything we had was on credit. I dreamed of a day when our home and land would be our own.

"All this sounds so negative. It even sounds as if we were poor. But the fact is, we had as much as anyone else. Now that I think of it, most of those who share this nursing home with me would probably agree, 'those were the good old days.'

"There were happy times. I shall never forget our first home, having a baby, and raising our first crop. Now that I think about it, the good old days were really no different than today."

With a tear, she reached out her hand. I gently squeezed it as I leaned over to kiss her. I then spoke into my dictaphone.

"Today is November 9, 1989. And this concludes my interview with Mrs. Thomas Ira Spradlin—except for one thing. I'm proud to call this working woman my grandmother."

Getting INtouch

All these generations of women . . . together we make up 2.4 billion of the world's population. We live in different cultures. We speak different languages. And we have different ways of life. Our lives are a paradox. We are extremely different, yet alike. Did you know
- we still do most of the world's domestic work?
- we provide more health care services than all of the organized health services combined?
- we grow one-half of the world's food?
- we make up over one-third of the world's paid labor force?

As a woman born in the early 1950s, I cannot help wondering if I am more like my mother or my grandmother. As I join the ranks of other working women of the 1990s, I find myself grasping for common threads that will tightly weave my life to the strong and durable fabrics of my mother's and grandmother's lives.

As I trace each thread, I am startled to realize that I may have more in common with my grandmother than my mother. Why? Sociologists suggest that simply being a working woman makes my life patterns more like my grandmother's than my mother's.

As far as my mother is concerned, she has little in common with either my grandmother or me. Yet, while sociologists believe that women my age do have more in common with their grandmothers than mothers, I am convinced that there are still vast differences when the patterns of our lives are compared. To be sure, I checked an American history textbook.

After close inspection, I was convinced that women in

the early 1900s differed significantly in their life-styles and family patterns from both their mothers and daughters. Equally, those born in the 1920s and 1930s also differed significantly from the generations before and after them. For example, women born during the depression years had their first child sooner after marriage and they were less likely to divorce than either their mothers or their daughters. In fact, during the 1950s marriage and family were clearly the dominant forces in their lives. While these are only "paper facts," they do paint a clear portrait of my mother!

My family was a typical upper middle-class family with a mother who worked at home and a father whose professional employment fit the stereotypical "Donna Reed" environment.

Like other families in my neighborhood, Dad brought home the bacon. Mother cooked it. Unlike her mother, ironing wasn't hard labor for my mother; she even wore a dress while she ironed baby diapers!

With three kids and a dog, perhaps my family could better be described as a "Father Knows Best" outfit. We may have been the last kids on the block to get a hula hoop, but we were the first to get a dishwasher.

Modern amenities of the 1960s became my mother's servants. Time was plentiful compared to the discretionary time of my grandmother. Mother's priorities were exact. As a whole, nothing was more important to women in the 1950s and 1960s than their family, their house, and their work. Because of the priority placed on the family by that generation of women, my mother's life was proscribed by her family commitments to a greater extent than the generation preceding or following her.

During this period, women's employment was largely structured around the demands of their family roles. That is, women for whom continuous employment was not a necessity may have entered the labor force only until they entered the labor room.

Why did women of the 1950s and 1960s put such staunch

emphasis on their home and family? Why did they insist that all 75 million baby boomers (children born after World War II and before the Beatles landed at JFK International Airport) have it all? Could the answer in part be a reflection of what these women wished for themselves when they were children?

Born in 1930, my mother had fewer material possessions than my generation. Yet, her family was far from poor. These were depression years and certain household items were scarce. While many modern amenities had been invented, some had been put on hold until America got on its feet again. And being the country that we were, America made a remarkable comeback.

By now, all little girls who played house in the 1940s had a chance to have their dream come true. All they had dreamed of having for their play-like families in the 1930s they got for their real-life families in the 1950s: a husband with stable employment; a warm home with as many amenities as they could afford; and children who received all that they had done without in their depression-era childhood.

What impact did Mother's commitment and benevolence have on the millions of girl children born in the 1940s, 1950s, and 1960s? While I can speak only from my vantage point, I am convinced that my response to my mother's benevolent life-style may be the same as that of countless of thousands of others like me. My most consistent observation of my mother was that she was bored. It seemed to me that all she had to do was to cook and wait for Daddy to come home.

For these reasons I decided early that when I grew up I wanted a different life-style . . . a challenge. I wanted to work outside the home. Apparently I was not alone, for today over 56 million women have entered the labor force. That's about 200 percent more than the women of my mother's generation. Thus, the pendulum swings once more.

I can't help wondering if one reason so many women in

my generation joined the work force was to gain some control over their lives and the decisions affecting them? My point of view may well be influenced by thoughts and experiences related to my own childhood. Like 75 million other youngsters whose formative years embraced the 1950s and 1960s, my childhood was congested with change and insecurity. I had little control over the fast-moving world.

During those years I saw the Russian satellite *Sputnik* orbit the earth; I practiced hiding under school desks to avoid the cold war's nuclear threat. I watched the horrifying footage of a president being slain. As a teen I experienced the pressures of a sexual revolution. I witnessed nonviolent marches turn into racial clashes. I said good-bye to classmates going off to war. I witnessed students marching in campus protests and joining movements for women's liberation.

But as the 1970s gave birth to the 1980s, our country realized that the American family would never be the same again. Overnight, it seemed, boomers bloomed from hippies to yuppies—young urban professionals.

A second reason women my age may be seeking independence could be that there is safety in numbers. While most of my peers were born during the calm Eisenhower years, what wasn't calm was the way we were tossed into the middle of the most outrageous demographic boom ever to hit America—the baby boom.

Boomers are considered to have more clout than any generation preceding them. It is my opinion that much of the clout comes from the sheer magnitude of numbers. This massive segment will comprise 39.2 percent of the adult population by the year A.D. 2000. It is, therefore, evident that never has a generation had such impact or influence as have boomers.

For the most part, boomers feel they have absolutely nothing in common with the generations of women who came before them. Why? For starters, nearly half of the adult female population between ages 26 and 46 are single.

Unlike most of our mothers, we handle our own finances—including getting instant cash from convenient automatic tellers. We cook delicious precooked frozen meals in minutes in the microwave, or run by the drive-through window at one of the restaurants near the office. Our answering machines are a constant reminder that friends have "reached out and touched."

Such changes among women in America, both young and old, are as stark and sharp as any seen before. Young women are much more likely to be working, to be educated, to be working at better jobs, to be better paid, and to be more independent than their mothers. The portrait of female independence exhibits many colors. If one talks about young women living alone, it can all sound rather exhilarating. Independence includes later marriage, more education, and fewer children. All of these tend to set in motion still other trends—ones that are not nearly as colorful. The trends of female headed households, women and children living in poverty, women caring for aging parents as well as for children and grandchildren are painfully real. They are not going away anytime soon. Where does that leave the American family of tomorrow?

In the 1980s we learned that having it all meant doing it all. Scores of women are now wistfully coveting a simpler time. Yet, perhaps, none of us are willing to turn back the clock.

It can be argued that these changes have been harmful. At the heart of the case is the idea that all those hearth-and-home women were sort of tricked into working, going to college, and having smaller families. Yet, many sociologists agree that the changes in the lives of today's women have occurred because American women decided they wanted to live differently than their mothers. Tens of millions of Americans apparently knew what they wanted and got what they wanted.

Getting Involved

As for me, I will never know all the answers. In fact, I may never fully know the questions. But one thing I do know. While my generation faces more changes than any other generation has faced, I submit that we still do not stand alone. My mother, grandmother, and I, all women of the 1990s, must embrace one another as we enter the twenty-first century. And, while my life is not like my mother's or my mother's mother's, I still share some of their priorities. The priorities which we share and continue to hold dearest are our family, our home, our church, and our work.

Together we are the women of faith in the 1990s. We are growing in more than numbers. But our options and opportunities are not without their oppressions. How we respond to life in the 1990s will affect not only the society in which we live but the kingdom of God which we represent.

It has been said that it is easier to know where we are going by first knowing where we have been. Now is the perfect time to see the truth of that statement. Let's pause for a brief moment in order to gain significant insights regarding where we are today by contrasting our lives with that of our mothers, grandmothers, and even great-grandmothers. Use the space below to record your answers. Write at least one sentence to describe each characteristic listed. If you are unsure about your answers, use this opportunity to interview key women in your family as means of gaining important insights regarding how life used to be for them.

THE WAY LIFE USED TO BE   THE WAY LIFE IS
Education

Home Life

Work/Career

Money

Faith

2

Countdown into the
Twenty-first Century

Boast not thyself of tomorrow, for thou knowest not what a day may bring forth.

Proverbs 27:1 (KJV)

She stood gracefully in front of her bedroom mirror. Carefully she applied last-minute touches of makeup to her ivory skin. Her scarlet red hair casually swept across her forehead.

She is beautiful, I thought. It seems impossible for her to be 13 today. Yet, something doesn't seem just right. When did she change from that little girl who loved dolls and writing her name with crayons into this young woman who takes life so seriously? It seems like magic; overnight she has been transformed.

I do miss holding her in my arms. But I must admit, I treasure each moment when she embraces me with her love. I can't escape wondering what her life will be like in five or ten years. And what will she contribute to the lives of others? The 1990s clearly hold the answers. While her mother and I have had so many opportunities that our mother never had, my niece Brooke will encounter more life opportunities than I can imagine.

Will she be a teacher like her mom? An astronaut? A Supreme Court judge? A doctor? Or a mother who will influence, nurture, and mold the lives of two or three red-haired toddlers? Of course, she could become the world's finest garbage collector! The jury is still out. Only time will unfold Brooke's life story.

I wish I could help her grow up. If only I could get inside of her and direct her thoughts and dreams. If only I could go before her and protect her from the tragedies of life in a world surrounded with drug abuse, AIDS, abortion, violence, homelessness, poverty, and emotional distress. Perhaps my dream is not unlike the dreams of any adult who cares so deeply for a child who is letting go of youth only to enter a world which isn't made of paper dolls and castles.

Brooke received many gifts on her birthday wrapped in colorful paper and sealed with love. If only I could give her something different, something that she cannot hold in her hands but embrace in her heart, something that would prepare her for her life ahead. What would it be? I would give her wisdom to know that it is not failure or success that matters in the final reckoning, but courage.

Where will Brooke find such courage? Only as she takes His word as her own. "Be on your guard, [Brooke]; stand firm in [your] faith; be [a young woman] of courage; be strong. Do everything in love" (1 Cor. 16:13 NIV [author's paraphrase added]).

Getting INtouch

Courage will count as we walk through the future that for so long has been characterized by uncommon confusion. Imagine! In a little less than ten years the century that has for so long existed in science fiction will become reality.

Like all new decades, the 1990s invite reflection, prediction, warning, and hope. Real life, of course, rarely fits neatly into little squares like days on a calendar. Yet there are compelling reasons to see the new decade as different than the ones that have gone before it.

What will our lives be like as we approach A.D. 2000? I believe those who are prepared will find unprecedented opportunity. After a long and tedious journey, our arrival into the future could mean we discover treasures of truth that illuminate hearts, souls, and imaginations. Annie Armstrong, a nineteenth-century supporter of missions, said, "The veil over the future is one of God's tenderest mercies." While we cannot literally move forward or backward in time, we can lift a corner of the veil and peek into the future.

As we wait for the twenty-first century to dawn, staggering changes begin to unfold before our eyes. Already books, newspaper and magazine articles, and television documentaries predict that our arrival into the twenty-first century will be characterized by what futurist Alvin Toffler called future shock. Future shock describes the shattering stress and disorientation that result from too much change in too short a period of time.

As we examine our perspective of the future, we put ourselves in a position to see the threads from which patterns are made. For thousands of years the threads of sameness characterized a person's life. It was not unusual for a person to be born and perhaps die in the same house. Likewise, it was common for nearly everything they knew to be just the same on the day of their death as on the day of their birth. The threads of sameness began to unravel with the birth of the Industrial Revolution.

Slowly, almost imperceptively, threads began to change their color, shape, and texture. As we stand at the threshold of the twenty-first century, the most colorful thread-weaving pattern in our lives is called change.

Most threads are colorful, radiant, and full of beauty. Unfortunately some are not. Can we, the explorers of this tenth decade, have some control over the changes surrounding us? Absolutely! That is, if we are willing to recognize the changes before us. Through awareness we can choose to weave these threads of change into a magnificent pattern. And the patterns we weave today may well become the trends of tomorrow. As the weavers, we must examine each thread. Will we weave patterns that radiate hope for the lost and homeless world? Or will the patterns we weave lack clarity and commitment? Perhaps you agree with the belief that we cannot affect the future. Yet to those of us living in the information age a passive outlook isn't good enough. In fact, knowledge of the future is about the most important thing we can obtain.

Recognizing future trends and issues as well as futuristic plans to augment them is imperative for all persons who wish to have an impact on this decade and beyond. Can we really track tomorrow's trends? Can anyone really forecast the future? Already social scientists are carefully weighing and analyzing today's world issues and trends in an effort to clarify tomorrow's future.

While it is true that many predictions are based on scientific data, it is important to realize that no human has the power to see around the bend. Now is the only time for us. In spite of our human limitations, there are ways we can make the future become a time of unprecedented opportunities.

How, you ask?

Awareness!

While raw numbers are sometimes difficult to put into perspective, we must if we are going to get a clear picture of where we are headed. What we must pay close attention to are the vital statistics that are shaping the future of over 237 million people in our nation.

Slowly, through observation seen only by the trained eye, these facts develop into the trends that are having an impact on the way we live now and the way we are going to live as we embrace the twenty-first century. By being keenly aware of the threads that are being woven by our society, we, women of faith, can prepare to become effective ministers, touching the lives of those living in our world in days to come.

While there are hundreds of trends that we could examine, I have chosen only a few for our inspection. These trends, I think, serve as a foundation on which hundreds, maybe thousands, of other trends and countertrends will be built during this tenth decade.

21

As we peek underneath the veil of the future, we must first prepare ourselves to expect the unexpected. In fact, nothing will be more consistent in the days to come than change. Neither you or I will be exempt from the impact of change coming and going at such a rapid clip that what seemed to be scientific today will be out-of-date tomorrow.

Change is not new to us. A close inspection of our history books reveals the excessive changes occurring over the past 50 years. According to futurologists, change isn't expected to go out-of-style. In fact, we may soon enter the greatest period of change the world has ever known.

Is it an exaggeration to think that we are now living through a second Industrial Revolution? I think not. Americans are impressed with the speed and depth of change around us.

Consider this: If you were born near or before the 1920s, you were born in the middle of human history. Almost as much has happened to the human race since you were born as happened in all the millennia before you were born. In our lifetime the boundaries have literally burst. The acceleration of change in our time has become an elemental force with personal, psychological, as well as sociological consequences. These elements of change hold within them an excitement coupled with dread.

A second trend impacting us now and in days to come is our throwaway society. Think about it. Objects pass into and out of our lives at a rapid pace. Tissues, towels, diapers, baby bibs, cameras, nonreturnable soda bottles, and paper wedding gowns are a few such items. Corn muffins can now be baked in throwaway tins. TV dinners are cooked and the containers trashed. Our homes have become large processing plants through which objects flow, entering and leaving faster than the speed of light. From birth to death we are inextricably embedded in a throwaway society.

Third, we must brace ourselves for the paradox of good and bad. While one may view her life as filled with happiness and contentment, her brother might well view his world as one of heartache and sadness.

Uncommon change; quick-fix, throwaway society; and a world where opportunities are tightly woven with oppression are trends that may well describe our world tomorrow. While the issues and trends of the 1990s do not all translate into joy and good will, barring no major disaster the 1990s do promise to be an intriguing and fluid decade. As I anticipate the future, I am reminded of the words of an old familiar hymn, "I don't know who holds tomorrow, but I know who holds my hand."

During the months of work necessary for writing this book, I found myself charged with energy, especially when researching future trends. In fact, it was not unusual for me to get so caught up in the mystery of tomorrow that I would forget or ignore the realities of today. It is imperative that we never get so caught up in tomorrow that we fail to live today, for now is the only time we have. What is happening in my world this moment is my only present reality.

As I write, I am keenly reminded of the unforeseen developments in Eastern Europe. As special news bulletins interrupted television programming on the eve of this tenth decade, people in every corner of our world quickly scrambled in an effort to readjust their ideologies to the new realities. Who among us would have ever predicted that the iron curtain separating the two Germanys would have crumbled in our lifetime?

Since none of us can escape the fact that the human experience is filled with unknowns, none of us can forecast with total accuracy what is to come. But we can have an impact on tomorrow by the choices we make today. Because of the need to be INtouch with our world today, perhaps it would be wise to let go of our expectations and dreams for a moment and take a careful look at our world today. Did you know

- there are in the US an estimated 20,000,000 problem drinkers, most of whom are alcoholics?
- approximately 5,000,000 people use cocaine regularly?

- as many as 10,000,000 people use marijuana regularly?
- there are 800,000 heroin addicts in the US?
- 1,100,000 teenaged girls in the United States get pregnant each year? A growing number are age 15 or under.
- over 100,000 people in the US have been diagnosed with AIDS?
- it is estimated that 90 percent of teenaged fathers will eventually abandon their children?
- the average woman seeking an abortion in the US can be profiled as white, 19 years old, single, never pregnant before?
- poverty affects 2,100,000,000 of the world's people, with 800,000,000 of them living in absolute poverty?
- the number of people in the US living below the poverty level is over 32,500,000, or nearly 14 percent, of the population?
- a divorced mother's available income drops 73 percent in the first year after the divorce, while the father's available income rises 42 percent?
- single women make up 14 percent of the homeless in the US?
- only 10 percent of the households in the US consist of a working father, a housewife mother, and children younger than 18?
- more than half of the divorced mothers receive no child support from their former husbands and few receive the full amount awarded by the court? Forty-one percent of the single mothers who receive no child support live in poverty with their children.
- two-thirds of the world is non-Christian?
- 69 percent of America's population is not Christian?
- the number of Christians in the world must grow by 2,800,000 a year just to keep pace with current population growth rates?

If you answered yes to all statements listed above, you are INtouch with your world. However, being INtouch with our world alone will not make a difference. We must be involved. I am confident that to the proportion we are involved in our world in Christ's name today, we are changing our world for Christ tomorrow.

What are we waiting for?

Getting Involved

By now you have realized that trends seem to indicate that the future will hold more opportunities than ever for the Christian woman to demonstrate courage. Yet while many of the trends and social concerns present a dim view of the future, as Christians we have the right to be enthusiastic about where we are headed. As we lift the corner of the veil into our future, perhaps we should begin to think, How will I take advantage of opportunities just outside my window?

Touching the lives of those living in our world in this new decade demands that both Christian men and women let go of their past limitations in order to grasp all that is fresh and new. As Sam Crowell pointed out, newness of thinking challenges us not to abandon dearly held values but to create a fuller vision of humanity's potential.

Please realize that the trends and issues just discussed, both the beneficial and the bleak, are meaningless except in the light of our relationship to Jesus Christ. As we ask ourselves, How will I respond and what can I do now to change or reverse trends which seem so bleak?, we put ourselves in the position of a responsible global citizen instead of a victim of prediction. With Christ we can live lives of results instead of excuses.

Reread the trends described on pages 21-24. Take as much time as you need to examine these "paper predictions." Out of all the predictions listed, select five. Write a statement describing the prediction in your own words in the space below. Using your most creative thinking, ask yourself, What can I do to turn the tide? What are the implications?

25

Complications? Think in both present and future tense. Be positive but realistic.

TREND OR ISSUE	WHAT I CAN DO
1.	
2.	
3.	
4.	
5.	

If you have completed the exercise above, you have seen that you can touch your world for Jesus Christ, regardless of how bleak the circumstance.

You are now ready for "Part II: Confronting Life's Changes, Choices, and Crises." The chapters contained in part 2 focus on key issues and trends which are directly touching women. As you read, you will become even more aware of the stark realities affecting our world. Coupled with these realities are women just like you and me—women who have chosen to raise their candles on high, imbuing enthusiasm, and reaching out to touch those whose lives are complicated or victimized by the realities of life.

As we explore the many trends facing women in the 1990s, may we remember that we are actually looking at the fields in our own back yard. May we realize that they are ripe and ready to be harvested by you and me, women of faith. Let us not waver or waste a moment.

PART II

CONFRONTING LIFE'S CHANGES, CHOICES, AND CRISES

3

Closing the Image Gap

*Humans live in time . . . therefore . . . attend chiefly to two
things, to eternity itself, and to . . . the Present. For the Present
is the point at which time touches eternity. . . . In it alone
freedom and actuality are offered.*
                                        C. S. Lewis
                                The Screwtape Letters

Recently I stopped by the grocery store on the way home
from the office. I needed to pick up only a couple of items
for my next day's breakfast. Since I was short on cash, I
simply wrote a check for $10.00 over the amount of pur-
chase. That was my first mistake. I trust I am not alone in
intensely disliking having to empty the intimate contents of
my purse on the grocery counter in order to find my driver's
license and two major credit cards. Everyone knows it is
impossible to get a check cashed unless you have credit
cards to prove you are already in debt.

Like most of you, I tried to remain patient as I stuffed
back into my purse a few dozen items necessary for con-
ducting my daily life: two tubes of lipstick, six-year calendar,
checkbook, calculator, compact, last year's Christmas gift
list, brush, three sticks of gums, two pens. . . . Wait a
minute. Where's the money? Isn't that the purpose in carrying this ten-pound bag in the first place? Thank goodness
for checking accounts, automatic tellers, and plastic money!
Regardless, I thought, I think it's time to get a bigger purse
or get new priorities.

I continued to wait while my cashier rubber-stamped the

back of my check in order to squeeze my life history into a one-inch box. The atmosphere was far from tranquil. The sound of cash registers' beeps, blurps, and bells was punctuation as she announced loudly enough for all persons within 100 feet to hear, "Miss Spradlin, you're old enough to be my mother!"

Trying to camouflage my emotions, I smiled while my stomach sank. To defend my youth I quickly responded, "Your mother must have been very young when she had you."

"Not really. I think Mom was at least 21."

"And how old are you?" I asked.

"Sixteen next month."

What could I say? Fortunately, the bag boy made my escape possible as he placed my $21.19 bag of groceries into my arms.

As I raced home, I tried to calculate how old I would have been when she was born. Ouch! She was right.

With a bag of groceries clutched under one arm, I quickly slipped the key into the door. As soon as I dropped the grocery bag, I dashed to my bedroom where there was a full-length mirror. After one quick glance, I got closer to the mirror to make sure what I was seeing. There it was. I wondered why I had never noticed it before. Underneath my eyes was an authentic wrinkle. I checked my neck. All women know that the neck goes first. Horrors! Right again. There was a little sagging. I guess it is true what they say: Time marches on. But in my case, I could not help feeling that time had marched across my face!

Relax, I thought. Time is no respecter of persons. But why couldn't it respect me just a little? After all, I don't feel that old. It seemed only moments ago that I thought turning 40 meant it was time to start selecting a nursing home. Surely there is something I can do. If only I could break the hourglass. Maybe then I would have time to catch up with myself, or at least recognize who I have suddenly become.

At bedtime I was bombarded and terrorized by my own thoughts. Am I that vain? Well, maybe a little. But wanting to cling tightly to my youth is part of being a woman. Everyone knows that life belongs to the young. Wait a minute. When did I began to associate who I was with how I looked, or even greater, what I did? But, is it so wrong to strive toward personal excellence? Isn't wanting it all a part of the American Dream?

In an effort to quiet the idea of losing my indestructible, youthful grip, I challenged myself to devise a plan. Surely there was something I could do to at least combat the symptoms. After all, when the going gets tough, the tough go shopping. That's it. All I needed was a more contemporary closet. I could start by replacing my starched, button-down shirts and career suits with something a little more upbeat. A couple of pairs of those designer jeans should do it.

And there was another thing. My car. Everyone knows that one's automobile is an extension of who they are. When I bought my midsize car four years ago, I wanted something a little more sophisticated, you know, grown-up. Even though it was paid for, there was no doubt that the expenditure for a new car could easily be justified.

Fortunately, recovery from an acute case of new car fever came quickly. With one glance at the sticker price of a car that promised to brighten my image, I recognized that both my car and I had to get in gear.

Driving home from the dealership, I wondered: How do people do it? My neighborhood is filled with men and women whose lives personify the perfect image of youth, health, and success. They appear to have it all. In my neighborhood, being in debt is a status symbol. There is no doubt that their wardrobes are financial statements of their success as well as their position on the economic ladder of life.

This image of success is everywhere. But where do these compelling statements of materialism come from? And why am I not exempt from the powerful force of commercialism? I wondered.

Recognizing that I too was easily caught up in the powerful image age was a sobering experience. I chose to step to the side in an attempt to understand why we so easily get caught in the trap of needing more and more to ensure our sense of worth. I started by driving across town.

What I saw caused dreadful remorse. There, just ten minutes from my home, which is nestled in an upper middle-class neighborhood, were hundreds of families sharing a single block. Malnourished children playing in sewers caused me grief and guilt. Yet in the middle of their poverty stood dozens of billboards with messages of how to obtain health, happiness, and prestige.

Let's face it. Commercialism is everywhere. Its messages are cunning, constant, and convincing. It's called the image age. And its purpose is to make us uncomfortable or discontented with our lives. Where does commercialism come from? Advertisements. Paraded across magazine racks, stuffed in our overcrowded mailboxes, heralded by unsolicited phone calls, sandwiched inside our newspapers, pasted on billboards on our highways, written across our kids' T-shirts, attached to our car bumpers, circumscribing baseball diamonds, and interrupting our television programs are messages; powerful messages to buy me, use me, taste me, and smell me.

Advertising may very well be controlling our lives.

Curious to know how many unsolicited messages I received each day, I conducted a simple test. First, I flipped through the pages of a popular women's magazine, the type sold at checkout counters in nearly all grocery stores. Plastered across the four-color cover in bold red type was the headline 25 Ways to Slow Down Aging. Since I was the age of my cashier's mother, I decided to find out how I could slow down the aging process. I never dreamed it was possible to slow down aging.

I quickly flipped the cover in search of the table of contents. After flipping through nearly six pages of advertisements, I found the table of contents; yet nowhere could I find the article that promised to slow down aging. So I searched through all 187 pages of the periodical. I never found the article on aging, but what I did find in the magazine were 122 pages containing advertisements, leaving only 36 pages for articles. Later in the evening I added to the magazine advertisements 36 commercials I viewed during a 90-minute television broadcast. That brought my total up to a whopping 158 ads. To this total I added the 18 bumper stickers and 46 billboards I counted during my drive to the office the following morning. From the front page to the back page, from the Atlantic to the Pacific, the message is the same: Happiness and success belong to those who have. And the best way to make you want is to make you unhappy or dissatisfied with what you have or who you perceive that you are. The never-ceasing concentration of commercialism is one of the most powerful forces in the lives of Americans. It is no wonder that wanting to have all and become all things is considered to be part of the American Dream.

Americans are living proof that commercialism has sold us a bill of goods of what life should be like. I believe the image age is filled with myths, mirages, and half-truths. Think about the people in your world. If your world is like the world of others reading this book, you will agree that for the most part, life is simply not OK anymore.

As commercialism tightens its grip, we begin to believe that our lives could be OK if we buy a certain type of home, drive a certain kind of car, wear designer clothes, and drink only imported bottled water. As I have traveled throughout the United States, I have recognized this to be true in nearly every aspect of people's lives, whether it is how they want to live as a family, the positions they want to hold, or the kinds of jobs they wish to maintain. Even more startling is my observation that I, along with my Christians friends, am far from being exempt.

What impact does commercialism have on society, Christians included? Unfortunately, it is difficult to measure. Commercialism means living on plastic money and in a house made of glass. Likewise, it means pretending to be all things to all people at all times. It means living hollow lives where deluded thinking convinces its victims that they are indestructible. Slowly, almost imperceptively, they allow themselves to believe that all is well as long as the glass house isn't cracked. What we don't realize is that this type of thinking is not unlike the individual who believed he could jump off a 50-story building without being hurt. As he hurtled downward, he could be heard saying, "So far so good."

Wrong! This shortsighted and frantic thinking and behavior typifies the person who strives to obtain it all, youth included.

I am convinced that commercialism has failed to tell the whole story. Imagine you and I peek behind the television screen into the real lives of those who convincingly testify of health, happiness, and success. If we could, we might see a rather interesting scenario. After the lights are turned off and the cameramen go home, those who try to convince us that our lives are empty probably greet their own hollow lives. They too leap from possession to possession in search for fulfillment. Their lives are solid proof that money can buy only temporary thrills. What we don't see is that these same individuals, the ones whose rank in life personifies success, often drown themselves in alcohol or drugs to escape the vacuum in their hearts and minds.

While Americans are placing more importance on intangible aspects of our lives (family, friends, etc.), we continue to place emphasis on money and what it can buy us.

Perhaps you are asking, Is it really wrong to want to have more, achieve more, and do more? These are important questions which deserve careful attention if we wish to live full, meaningful, and productive lives in a world where "meism" is rampant. Could the fatal flaw in our value system be the result of inappropriate motivation? When our motivation stems from our dependence on "other" worth rather than self-worth, we become a deceived victim, one whose good is dependent on something, someone, or somewhere.

Think about that. If we choose to identify our good with what we have, we set ourselves up to experience deep feelings of lack and limitation the very moment we reach our credit limit on our charge cards. If we choose to identify our good with where we are, our happiness caves in the moment we are no longer there. If we choose to identify our good with who we are with, we set ourselves up for loneliness the moment he or she goes away. Can the chains of commercialism be broken? Not only do I believe the answer is yes, I believe you can have it all, all that really matters, if you do it right. Interested? Read on.

Getting INtouch

There is a great and vast distance between having anything you desire and having everything you desire. We would be wise to recognize that the emphasis of victims of the image age is obtaining everything. Such wants and needs are not unlike walking through a revolving door which never stops.

Could the problem be that we are unsure of what we want out of life? What *do* Americans want out of life? In a recent issue of "Research Information Report" (a monthly review of demographic, social, and religious trends) a significant shift in what Americans desire was reported. While intangible elements (happy marriage, children, a satisfying job, etc.) remain as dominant elements in the good life, material aspirations figure more prominently in people's ideas of what makes up the good life. The report goes on to say that "today, 62 percent of Americans feel that a lot of money is necessary for the good life."

Components of the Good Life

ELEMENTS	1988	1981
A home that you own	86%	83%
A happy marriage	77%	79%
A car	72%	64%
Children	72%	69%
A lot of money	62%	43%
A job that is interesting	61%	61%
A job that pays much more than the average	61%	45%
A yard and lawn	60%	55%
A college education for my children	59%	54%
A color TV set	56%	40%
A second car	46%	28%
Travel abroad	45%	36%
Really nice clothes	44%	33%
A college education for myself	43%	36%
A vacation home	42%	25%
A job that contributes to the welfare of society	35%	29%
A swimming pool	34%	18%
A second color TV set	29%	12%
A four-day work week	26%	18%
No children	3%	2%[1]

In essence, Americans still want it all. And, while it is important to enjoy what you have, it is also important to grow from where you are. I am convinced that we can't get a grip on what we need or where we need to be until we fully appreciate what our Father has given us, as well as where He has placed us. In other words, before we can fully know and appreciate where we are going, we must first know where we are.

Could it be that we don't want to know where we are

because we are painfully aware that we are in the wrong place and headed in the wrong direction? Could it be that we dread looking at what we already have in fear of being reminded of what others have not? We must stop at all cost and study our dissatisfaction carefully. As we do, we put ourselves in a position to learn something incredible about ourselves. But, just as an internal inventory is not without pain, an inspection of our external world is equally discomforting and oftentimes distasteful.

Regardless of the discomfort, I know of nothing that brings clarity into my life as does counting my blessings. Stop. Look around. Like countless others, you may have been too consumed with consuming to have noticed all that the Father has given you.

Let's look at our world together and compare our situation with the facts listed below. Did you know

- between 1978 and 1985 the number of Americans working full time but living below the poverty line increased by 50 percent?[2]
- approximately two-thirds of all poor workers do not receive health insurance?[3]
- the average US annual pay in 1988 was $21,871?
- the 1988 annual minimum wage salary was $536 a month, yet child-care costs alone were an average $228 a month per child nationally?[4]
- almost half of the working poor women are high school graduates?[5]

Getting Involved

While the facts and trends are stark and sharp, who among us can afford to simply look away? In a world where poverty, hunger, and hurt prevails, there is an urgent plea for relief. Who will respond to the cry? Certainly not those whose lives are weak and withering away. I submit to you that only those priceless women of faith who have bravely let go of their image of lack and limitation to make room for an image of true spiritual abundance in Jesus Christ will find the necessary resources to touch the lives of our hungry and hurting world. Such images of abundance starts as we recognize who we are in Jesus Christ.

Our lives and our world are ever-changing canvases. What are we going to paint on the canvases of our lives? Are you going to paint a life of lack and limitation? If you do, you will most likely reap lack and limitation. Or are you going to paint a life fulfilled, abundant, and complete?

Perhaps the shock of spiritual self-discovery is realization that our Father's plan for our lives includes abundance and a pursuit for excellence. In these challenging times, it is urgent that women of faith strive to become all that they can become in Jesus Christ. We must realize that a life-style of spiritual excellence isn't the same as self-centered perfection that brings the world's acclaim. God does not expect instant spiritual perfection. He expects obedience. And to the degree that we are obedient He can turn our failures into triumphs and limitations into abundance.

"But where do I start?" you ask. The major key to a life abundant in Christ is you—not your boss, not your salary, not your situation. I believe living the abundant life starts with a vision, a vision of the person God has called you to be, the work He has given you to do. Have faith that what He has called you to do, He will equip you to do.

"I'm not ready," you say. "You don't know my case."

The biggest game in town is to pretend that we are victims of the world we see and have no responsibility for what is happening to us or around us. Our motto may well be, If anything can go wrong, it will; and even if it can't, it still might. Our lives are living testimonies of excuses which take the place of a life-style of result. "I can't make it Sunday. I have to work on Wednesday night. I can't afford to take the time."

Yet one week later when the house burns down, we suddenly realize that we do have the time for the things and people we care about most. It is a matter of priorities.

Priorities begin with our purpose in life. It is the spiritual priorities that are most often neglected and so easily forgotten in the crush of external demands. But in the final analysis, the bottom line, it is the internal priorities, the spiritual ones, that really count.

I believe our Father gives us the freedom to choose. If the choice is mine, I much prefer the abundant life. But before I can have such a life, I must realize what the abundant life is not.

An abundant life is not one filled with materialism, wealth, and glitter. It is not associated with age, race, or status on the economic ladder. It has nothing to do with where I live or who I am with. And it has little to do with what I do—my job, profession, or career.

Instead, the abundant life is about Whose I am. The abundant life is not about being better than your neighbor. Instead, it is about being better than yourself through Jesus Christ. The moment we realize that our Father is Creator of all things is the beginning of change in our wants and wishes. And in the reflective space where my wants and wishes once dwelled is the realization that I am an heir, a member of God's royal priesthood. All that is His is mine. He has given me spiritual gifts in order to conduct His business. He gives me the fruit of His Spirit to nurture my life and glorify His name. What freedom is mine the moment I realize that I no longer have to strive to have. Instead, my value comes from God. I am called to do His will. My purpose is enhanced and my priorities clarified.

"But my life is a mess," you say. Paul Tournier, the well-known Swiss psychiatrist, has said that God's plan works not just through our obedience but also through our errors. The Bible is replete with examples of how God turned people's failures—and forgiven sins—into great triumphs.

If you are serious about turning the tables on a life-style where only lack and limitation reside, I submit to you to prayerfully prepare a plan. Likewise, our churches would do well to address materialism and help persons establish proper priorities. Through spiritual guidance, we must devise a plan for proper use of the material wealth the Father has entrusted to us. Likewise, we must trust the Father as we experience the frustrations of not achieving the good life as society has defined it.

The time is now. The infinite needs surrounding us are calling all women to proclaim His magnificence. But choosing the path of spiritual abundance in order to touch our world with His greatness is not without risk. Remember the turtle; he makes progress only when he sticks his neck out. It is true. We will never stub our toe standing still. Likewise, we touch the lives of the spiritually weak and economically malnourished the moment we are willing to "walk in wisdom toward them that are without, redeeming the time" (Col. 4:5 KJV).

How will you proclaim His magnificence in an age where self-fulfillment and gratification are the biggest games in town? In the space below write at least three ways you plan to turn the tide of commercialism.

[1]"Cliff Tharp, comp., "Research Information Report," series 4, no. 13 (Nashville: Baptist Sunday School Board, August 1989).

[2]"Research Alert" 6 (April 28, 1989):7.

[3]Ibid.

[4]Ibid.

[5]Ibid., 8.

4

Facing Addiction

The Lord's curse is on the house of the wicked, but he blesses the home of the righteous.
Proverbs 3:33 (NIV)

Nothing is more wonderful or dreadful than families. I doubt that anyone understands this point of view more clearly than Jessie Martin. For her, nothing was more wonderful than her loved ones. To all who knew them, theirs was the perfect family. Jessie and her husband, John, had three healthy children and a beautiful home in which to love and nurture them.

In many ways, Jessie was no different than her friends. Like most women starting their families in the 1950s, Jessie's goals were simple. "I wanted my husband and children to know how much I loved them. I did this by providing what I felt was a home which nurtured love." But what Jessie wanted and what she got did not prove to be the same.

Her story is as painful as any I have ever heard. It is a story of unconditional love, the kind of love only found in a family. In a brief interview with Jessie, she shared her experience.

"My story is painful, so painful that never a day goes by that I don't cry. But I believe that those who are not killed by their pain have the chance to grow from it. This does not mean that one seeks pain. Rather it means that one looks to the Father as the only relief in times of need. And, believe me, being the mother of three children whose lives are as

41

complicated and complex as any I have ever seen, I do have many opportunities to exercise trust."

I knew Jessie's words were true and sincere. A life-threatening experience of my own had permanently inscribed on my heart and mind that we can grow in proportion to the pain we are willing to accept—not choose, but accept.

"I first noticed my daughter's problem when she was still a teenager. Julie had decided that she wanted to get married. But she was so young. Both my husband and I insisted that she finish school. In spite of our wishes, Julie did get married.

"One year later Julie had her first child. It was then that her problem began to mushroom. Suddenly Julie was faced with the responsibility of a child. She rebelled against being tied down by becoming even more of a free spirit than before.

"On one occasion I spoke with Julie's doctor regarding her competence in caring for her child. He was convinced that my beautiful Julie was both loving and capable. But I know my daughter.

"Soon after the baby came Julie got involved in drugs and prostitution. She was in and out of jail. You might think that knowing your daughter is on drugs and engaging in prostitution would be the hard part. But for me, the hardest part was not knowing where she was or even if she had food to eat.

"Julie's first run-in with the law was regarding the sale of marijuana. I am convinced that Julie was not guilty. She was set up. Her husband first got her high on drugs and then used her to make the sales. When Julie was caught, it was Julie who was prosecuted by the state, not her husband. Julie was sentenced to 13 years in the state correctional center. Because the correctional center was overcrowded, Julie spent the first 13 months in the county jail in our city. Her baby ended up being adopted by her in-laws.

"I shall never forget my first trip downtown to visit Julie in jail. People were crammed into small rooms awaiting inspection. I felt rather intimidated at first. I felt I had nothing in common with the hundreds of people lined up to see their loved ones. They were not exactly the kind of people I associated with. In fact, these people made the welfare lines look like the Ritz.

"I eventually realized that I did indeed have something in common with the people crammed shoulder to shoulder in that small room. We each had a loved one on the other side of the fence.

"Every Friday morning I joined the ranks of hundreds of other people who desperately sought even a glimpse of their loved one. I left each visit with tears streaming down my cheeks. I was not alone. Many others left the county jail in the same emotional state of fear, anger, and hopelessness.

"Never in the 56 consecutive Friday morning visits did I not recognize God's presence. His presence came in the form of a compassionate prison guard. After my visit with Julie, the guard would invite me to sit in his office to regain my composure before leaving my only daughter in that cold concrete jail. I always wondered, Of all the hundreds of people crowding into the prison, why did the guard choose to minister to me?

"Each visit grew harder. Julie would beg me to find a way to get her out of jail. But regardless of how difficult the visits were, I continued to see Julie every Friday. With each visit I found myself juggling my role. During each drive home from the prison, I would ask myself, Am I Julie's mother or am I a citizen? Is Julie my daughter or is she a criminal? It wasn't easy for me to realize that the answer wasn't one or the other. The answer was both. I was the mother of a criminal.

"After 13 months Julie was released on an appeal bond (that is where two people had to agree to put their property up for bond). My husband and a physician friend signed the forms. The courts allowed Julie to be out on bail only until her trial. When her appeal was denied, I had a terrible feeling that she had skipped. When my husband went to get Julie in order to turn her over to the authorities, Julie had skipped. That meant we, as well as our physician friend, could have lost all.

"During the time she was out on bond, Julie had gotten pregnant. She was well into her fifth month when she skipped bail. These were difficult days. We did not know where she was, much less if she had food to eat. In my own defense, I continued to insist that Julie loved us and was aware that we cared very much. In fact, I was confident that Julie knew we were mortified, especially since we knew about the baby. Yet I realized she couldn't tell us where she was, not as long as the authorities were looking for her.

"Eight months passed without a word from Julie. My prayer had been, If only she could send a card, something to let us know she is alive. My prayer was answered one afternoon as I gathered the mail from the mailbox. Stuffed in between bills and advertisement pieces was a small envelope. I knew the writing well. Like any mother, I dropped the mail as I ripped into the envelope with no return address. It said

Dear Mom:
I am fine.
Here is a picture of your four-month-old granddaughter.
      Love, Julie

"Eleven months passed without a clue as to where Julie was, much less how she was. Those were the most depressing days I had. Part of my depression may have been the fact that I had just had major surgery. Having to stay in bed only gave me more time to think about Julie. Every day seemed the same. Each morning I grasped for hope. Each afternoon I would feel my hope sinking as I returned from the mailbox empty-handed.

"Yet on one of those rather dull, gray days my life drastically changed. The shrill ring of the telephone broke the silence of the day. The call was from a woman in Houston, Texas. I will never forget the words of that lady: 'Your daughter has been picked up by the authorities. I have her baby. I am sending her to you.'

44

"Please realize that I had never seen this child. Yet within a few hours my husband and I stood in the cold downtown bus station awaiting the arrival of the bus from Houston.

"The baby was beautiful . . . just like her mother. Her little eyes shone with hope. When her body was placed in my arms, I felt myself leaning into our Father's arms. I knew I would need His encouragement now, maybe more than ever.

"This time Julie was sentenced to Tutwiler Prison. For some reason, I expected Julie to turn herself around and to shape up. My husband and I very much wanted Kelly to know and love her mother. Of course, that meant exposing Kelly to prison life. Every three weeks John, Kelly, and I made the trip to Tutwiler. Visiting inside this facility was terrible. We were strip searched before we were allowed inside the prison compound. But once inside we always felt it was worth it. We would usually spend the entire day with Julie. After a while, Kelly began to know Julie as Mommy.

"When Kelly was four, Julie was released. She moved to Knoxville to live with her husband, who had also been released from prison. Kelly became confused. Julie wanted to see her baby. But as soon as Julie got tired of caring for Kelly, she would send her back to me.

"During this time Julie and her husband began to have problems. Julie left and moved closer to home. As much as I wanted to believe that Julie had kicked drugs, I had to face reality once more. My daughter was a drug addict. And a day never passed that I did not pray as I tried to imagine where she was and what she was doing.

"One night in particular comes to mind. The evening news claimed that the low that night would be only seven degrees. All I knew was that Julie had no money, nothing to eat, and probably not even a blanket.

"I learned later that Julie and her boyfriend had spent the night in a parked car. Julie was not only cold, she was hungry. That's when she and her friend entered a local grocery store and held a gun on a person in line who was writing a check for several bags of groceries. When the groceries were paid for, Julie took the bags and escaped. She carefully weeded out all items not needed.

"Her plan was to return these stolen goods to the grocery store for cash. This was her biggest mistake. Of course she was recognized. Julie was charged with first-degree robbery.

"I didn't go to Tutwiler during her second prison sentence. One reason was that my husband did not approve of my going. 'She is using you, Jessie; can't you see that?' John insisted. He was right. As long as I was there for her, she would continue to use me.

"My own conviction was the second reason I did not go back to the prison. Kelly needed a lot of attention. I began to feel that the best thing I could do for Julie was to love and nurture Kelly. It was during Julie's second prison sentence that John and I adopted Kelly.

"I could go on and on about Julie. You see, her story isn't over. Julie has had at least two more husbands and three other children. Except for her first baby and Kelly, all of her children have been placed in foster homes. Just weeks ago Julie celebrated her 40th birthday. I assume she celebrated alone. Even as I speak, I am overwhelmed with grief. I know it is grief that can make us strong. Yet I still ask why. And just when I think I can handle this whole mess, I have to realize just how much I need the Lord.

"I realize I am not the only woman in the world whose child turned bad. But what I also realize is that my pain and grief may have been my best teachers. On a small index card taped to my bathroom mirror are these words: Remember, Jessie, because of Jesus Christ, that which hurts can only make my faith stronger."

Getting INtouch

It is true. Nothing is more wonderful or dreadful than families.

Yet membership in a family is inescapable. You can reject it and denounce it, but you cannot resign from it. And while you choose your friends, for the most part, you don't choose the members of your family. Perhaps these are some of the reasons that one of the greatest concerns in America today is the family; for if the family fails, then all the other institutions of society will fail.

The family is the basic unit of society which undergirds all else. Therefore, every influence which weakens the family weakens society.

It must be noted that families don't just break up. There are reasons and issues that influence the break up. While there are numerous reasons for family crisis, perhaps the most important issue weakening the American family in the 1990s is substance abuse. No longer can Christians afford to simply put bandages on issues affecting the family; instead, it is necessary to get at the heart of the problem. We must be willing to ask ourselves, Will the family endure the turbulent days of the future? Let's take a closer look at this issue that is hitting close to home.

Who are the addicted? Until I met Jessie, I thought chemical addiction was isolated to the homeless alcoholics who sleep in alleys. Now I realize that 95 percent of the addicted are not Skid Row bums. They don't look like the stereotypical dirty, homeless wino. In fact, most are like Julie; they come from nice, respectable families.

It is becoming increasingly evident that chemical dependency influences us all in one way or another.

Health care professionals recognize that chemical dependency is not the same as in the past. Chemical dependency is now one of the American family's greatest problems. In fact, the American family is now in the middle of an epidemic of addiction that is spreading three ways.

First, it spreads geographically. Addiction crosses from urban into rural areas. Second, it spreads economically. Addiction has captured the lives of people in every income bracket. Third, it spreads chronologically. Addiction has hurt every age group from infants born addicted through their mothers' placentas, to elementary school children, to elderly residents drugging their lives away in retirement homes.

Nearly everyone knows at least one person who is addicted to drugs or alcohol. Unfortunately, many know them well; they are sharing the same home. Simply stated, drug abuse affects everyone in one way or another.

While federal- and state-funded programs are in place to encourage our youth to Just Say No to illegal drugs, another drug crisis is creeping into the American family. In her book *The Female Fix,* Muriel Nellis suggests that in the 1980s "one in every four American women is addicted to legally prescribed drugs—painkillers, tranquilizers, diet pills, and sedatives." And it often seems that the least suspecting among us is the most vulnerable.

Shocking statistics in the 1980s affirmed the great amount of prescription drugs used by women. Did you know

• a full 160 million prescriptions were written annually for tranquilizers, sedatives, and stimulants; and only about 10 percent were authorized by psychiatrists, the one group of doctors trained to monitor the effects of such drugs?

• depending on the drug classification—tranquilizers, sedatives, or stimulants—60 to 80 percent of all drugs prescribed were for female patients?[1]

Why women? Let's call it the female pattern of prescription drug abuse. While it is now clear that women as well as men are pursuing dangerous drug-using paths, health specialists and official regulators continue to focus on a male drug culture. This presumably benign oversight has permitted a malignant growth to go unchecked. We know while the rates of drug use are higher among men with both legal and illegal drugs, females are far more likely to obtain drugs through medical channels—prescriptions.

The National Institute on Drug Abuse is investigating the use of drugs and their effects on women. A federal research program has included on its study agenda the gender variables affecting drug use and abuse. According to *Women and Drugs: A New Era for Research* the following items are up for review.

48

• The use of stimulants by women, particularly young women wanting to lose weight
• Factors that account for higher levels of physician visits and prescriptions for women compared to men
• The effects of women's changing roles and increasing presence of women in the labor force
• The possible link between divorce and substance abuse[2]
Unfortunately, drug users are often able to hide their problem until it is too late. While many family members may suspect a chemical addiction, they prefer to adjust their own thinking rather than admitting the problem and taking responsibility for intervention. They then discover to their grief that their suspicions were right.

Getting Involved

Chemical dependency is not unlike a wrecking ball which is swinging into America's most cherished institution—the American family. Unfortunately, nothing in life can prepare us for the disasters that a chemical obsession unleashes within a family. The series of automobile accidents, arrests, breakups, batterings, bankruptcies, shattered dreams, heartaches, and bewilderment really do confront the family of the chemically dependent. As a result, emotions begin to disintegrate as each disaster unfolds.

If someone in your family has a drug or alcohol problem, the first thing you must realize is that there is always hope. Hope is often packaged in help. And help does work. But how can you be sure if your loved one really has a problem with drugs or alcohol?

Experts agree that few people live their lives as good, successful, sane individuals and then start behaving in drastically different ways—often to the point of being dysfunctional. The first step of intervention is to face up to the problem.

According to many experts in the field of dependency, the addict is one whose drinking or drugging interferes with one or more aspects of her life. If someone you care about is acting in a way that concerns you and you feel there is reason to believe he or she drinks or takes drugs, look at that issue first. The following questions may help you determine exactly how dependent your loved one could be. Answer each question on the basis of your observation of the person for whom you are concerned. Does your loved one

1. have the tendency to frequently oversleep?
2. withdraw from social functions, friends, and family?
3. appear to have difficulty concentrating?
4. do things or say things under the influence of alcohol or drugs that violates his or her own rules of behavior?
5. break promises to himself or herself about the use of alcohol or drugs?
6. pay an emotional price (shame, guilt, fear, remorse, self-directed anger, etc.) for using alcohol or drugs?
7. seem to have a different version of the drinking or drugging behavior than other witnesses?
8. become defensive, rationalize, or even lie if you ask these questions?[3]

If you answered yes to most of these questions, chances are strong that your loved one is indeed addicted. Only as you confront your loved one and agree to seek treatment is hope on its way. No matter how much you love your family member, you cannot make him or her change. Before your loved one can move toward recovery, he or she must accept the responsibility for the problem. And he or she must be held accountable.

Once the problem is identified, treatment begins with detoxification—ridding the body of the chemical substance that has been abused and allowing the body to adjust to not having the substance. It is important that detoxification is supervised by a qualified health care professional.

Detoxification needs to be followed by counseling. There are many agencies available in nearly every community that can guide your loved one through a recovery process and encourage you as you encourage the addicted.

Reread the list of characteristics on page 50. If someone you love is chemically dependent, decide now what action you are willing to take. Write your plan in the following space.

While books on how to act against addiction are available in nearly all bookstores, books and pamphlets cannot take the place of qualified treatment centers. As you read the following list of resources and treatment centers, circle at least one you will contact this week.[4]

• Hot line: The toll-free number for a national drug and alcohol abuse hot line is 1 (800) BE-SOBER.

• Cocaine treatment: The toll-free number for help with cocaine addiction is 1 (800) COCAINE.

• Treatment centers: There are alcohol and drug abuse treatment centers all over the country. The average hospital stay is two to three weeks, though it may be longer or shorter. Check the yellow pages for local listings.

• Alcoholic Anonymous: There are AA meetings in almost every area of our country. For more information write

Alcoholics Anonymous World Services
P. O. Box 459, Grand Central Station
New York, NY 10063

• Excellent books that openly confront the painful effects of addiction and the potentially healing effects of controlled confrontation include the following:

Crisis Intervention: Acting Against Addiction by Ed Storti and Janet Keller

Helping Women in Crisis by Kay Marshall Strom

Love Must Be Tough by James Dobson
Help to Get Help: When Someone Else's Drinking or Drugging Is Hurting You! by John and Pat O'Neill

[1]Muriel Nellis, *The Female Fix* (Boston: Houghton Mifflin Company, 1980; New York: Penguin Books, 1981), 5-6.

[2]Barbara A. Ray and Monique C. Braude, eds., *Women and Drugs: A New Era for Research*, National Institute on Drug Abuse, Research Monograph 65 (Rockville, MD, 1986), 97-98.

[3]John O'Neill and Pat O'Neill, *Help to Get Help: When Someone Else's Drinking or Drugging Is Hurting You!* (Austin, TX: Creative Assistance Press, 1989), 8.

[4]Kay Marshall Strom, *Helping Women in Crisis* (Grand Rapids, MI: Ministry Resources Library, 1986), 32.

5

Rejecting the Supermom Syndrome

Commit thy works unto the Lord, and thy thoughts shall be established.

Proverbs 16:3 (KJV)

"Our Mom is super. Even though she has a job, she still finds time for us," explained Teresa Persons's three children.

To her executive husband, she is a supportive wife as well as a world-class Christian mother.

"Teresa is one of Jackson Middle School's most dedicated, energetic, and compassionate teachers. She demonstrates genuine interest in each student, especially those with learning disabilities," explained principal Garrison.

Her students say, "Mrs. Persons bubbles with enthusiasm. She sees the best in us and always makes learning fun."

Teresa Persons's list of credentials are incalculable. I have often wondered how anyone could seemingly have it all—especially enough time to match her creativity.

Just listening to her describe her daily routine makes me exhausted. How does she juggle her many roles? I have difficulty juggling my career and personal life, which consists of washing one load of clothes per week, getting to work or the airport on time, and making sure my six plants are watered.

On the contrary, before Teresa launches into her demanding day, she must make plans for her family of five and her community and church activities, as well as preparing to teach 165 sixth-grade social studies students. With so many responsibilities you can see why Teresa must double-check her daily "to do" list on her refrigerator door.

To hundreds of thousands of women Teresa's organized life may be routine. But the compelling demand to be organized hasn't always been a necessity for Teresa. In fact, until five years ago Teresa claims that her life was rather mundane and lacking purpose.

Today Teresa joins the ranks of over 60 percent of married women with children aged 6 to 17 who have moved from the labor room into the labor force.[1] And like those who have gone before her, she is taking with her clarity and commitment.

I was so intrigued with the grace, confidence, and ease with which she greeted each day, I felt compelled to probe deeper into the life of this extraordinary woman.

I arose early one morning to drive the 275 miles to Mobile, Alabama, by noon. Prior to my trip, I contacted Paul Garrison, the school's principal, to inquire if I could observe Teresa in action. Not only did Garrison make arrangements for me to observe Teresa leading her students, he also arranged an interview with her during her free period.

I arrived just minutes before 11:00 A.M. The 600 students of Jackson Middle School were darting through the maze of hallways, elbow to elbow, shoulder to shoulder. The familiar sounds of locker doors opening and slamming, as well as tennis shoes squeaking, reminded me of my own junior high days. But there were some big differences.

"This certainly doesn't look like the junior high school I attended," I declared as Garrison escorted me to Teresa's class.

"If you think the hall environment is warm and inviting, wait until you see Mrs. Persons's room," Garrison explained.

Inconspicuously, I slipped into the back door of her third period social studies class. Garrison was right. The atmosphere was delicious. Instead of industrial-strength green walls, I saw color—bold, bright color—saturating the walls and covering every inch of what could have been a dull classroom. Mobiles hung from the ceiling, brightening corners. The bulletin boards underneath the classroom clock had been transformed into a collage displaying baby pictures of all 165 students. Dozens of green plants and flowers dotted the windowsill. Purposeful conversation punctuated the quiet. But something was missing. The teacher. Where is Teresa? I wondered.

My eyes scanned each cluster of students sitting at tables and desks. Finally, I spotted her sitting patiently at a table with a student—one struggling to grasp the meaning of her assignment written on the chalkboard.

I was enchanted with what I saw. My image of a teacher had just been shattered. Even though I was a teacher once (I retired after only one year), in my mind's eye the teacher was still supposed to be twice Teresa's age and size. I imagined someone with gray hair twisted into a tight little bun and held by two combs which never matched, wearing polyester dresses and lace-up black shoes.

Teresa was not what I had expected. Instead she looked more like a student than a teacher. This petite 5-foot 3-inch, 107-pound, 37-year-old Miss America look-alike was wearing jeans, a Mickey Mouse sweatshirt with matching wristwatch, white tennis shoes, and a curly bobbed haircut. When I later inquired why she dressed so informally, she replied, "Today's students have grown up in a world of entertainment. For the majority of their lives learning has been packaged in fun experiences—computers, video games, and other high-tech learning experiences. By dressing casually every once in a while, I hope to capture their attention. But this is not my only purpose in my occasional casual dress. I feel it contributes warmth that many of my students have never felt and it communicates the love I choose to give each one.

"But dress is not to be confused with respect. My students

respect me and they learn. Teaching respect comes not in how I dress but in how I handle myself and how I communicate my excitement, joy, and fear about everyday current events—learning! Of course, I do wear a suit and heels every couple of days just to make life interesting. I want my students to see more than one side of me. We are all multifaceted individuals. As I allow my students to know me, I feel they are more likely to be motivated to know what I know. Interestingly enough, because my students are products of the computer age, they occasionally know more than I do when it comes to technology. That's why I call myself the learning leader. Our motto is Learning Together.

After a couple of hours of observation, it was time for Teresa's free period. I pulled out my dictating machine and steno pad as we headed for a quiet corner in the teacher's lounge. There I continued asking questions. My main objective and interest was in learning how she juggled the many commitments and responsibilities of her life. Can a working mother with a productive yet demanding career maintain a family? In my journal I recorded these notes.

November 17

"Teresa, my sources are rather opinionated. They each insist that you are a supermom. But wasn't it just a few years ago that you struggled with your sense of worth? What happened? When did you become a supermom?"

"Marsha, you'll have to excuse my ignorance. I mean, I am not sure exactly what a supermom is. Of course, I've seen the television commercials which show women flying through life with the greatest of ease. But as far as I am concerned, *supermom* is a term used to describe those women who are all things to all people at all times. Frankly, I don't think that person exists. At least I've never met her. While it may appear that I am successfully juggling it all, the fact is that I join the ranks of all working mothers who struggle to juggle."

"When did you decide to join the ranks of the almost

60,000,000 working women?"

"Marsha, when I was growing up in the late 1950s and 1960s, I found myself on the tail end of the superhomemaker era and the front end of the working woman era. This presented quite a predicament. I was very confused as to which direction I wanted to go with my life. Half of me wanted to go to college and follow a career of teaching, but the other half wanted desperately to settle down and raise a family. I wanted a white picket fence, a dog in the back-yard, station wagon, and two or three children. To me this was the whole package. I followed the latter path. Please underscore that while I love my family and am extremely devoted to them, I must admit that I was never truly fulfilled. I became very tired of salesmen telling me that they would discuss the price of a car or carpet with me when I returned with my husband. Likewise, I grew weary of feeling like a second-class citizen when the grocery store cashier asked me my work telephone number. Running a house with three kids and a dog is real work. But it wasn't the kind of work our society had come to view as a legitimate career.

"When a woman has a family, the decision to work or not to work is incredibly difficult. I can't speak for any other women, nor can they speak for me. To work or not to work is a personal choice that must be made by a woman and her husband with leadership from God. No one can make that decision for you nor can anyone fully comprehend the pros and cons until they walk a week in your house shoes. It is truly a lesson in home economics.

"In my situation I didn't feel that I fit in anywhere. My husband and most of my friends had their degrees and careers. All of my life I had been an A student. But after three weeks of college, I called it quits. I had met Milt and all that was on my mind was marriage. I don't regret marry-ing Milt, but I do regret not completing my education before I had a family. All of my life education was one of the two most important priorities embossed in my heart and soul. Church was number one.

"During the first years of marriage, I had occasional part-time employment outside the home. That's when I really felt trapped. I felt guilty for not working and guilty for not being at home.

"After my babies were born, I continued to struggle. I loved my family, but I still felt something was lacking. Milt noticed. It wasn't long until he began to encourage me to take advantage of our community college by taking a couple of courses. Since I had always loved cooking, I decided to take cake decorating. For months I cooked cakes for every occasion. But after putting on 15 pounds, I decided that the cakes and 15 pounds had to go.

"That's when I enrolled in beauty school. I don't regret that decision. I still cut my children's hair. But working as a beauty operator wasn't me.

"Insurance was next. This was the biggest challenge ever. I knew that if I passed the exam, I could work while the kids were in school. The classes were exhilarating. And my little ones seemed to enjoy watching Mommy study and prepare for her test. They teased me: 'No TV, Mom, until all of your homework is done.' I did well on the test. In fact, I was the only woman in our region to ever make 100. Making 100 satisfied my goal, and that was the end of my career as an insurance agent.

"I hit the bottom after the regional insurance test. I had achieved everything I felt I could achieve, yet I still felt a hollow nagging feeling deep inside. What I didn't realize was that others were watching my vacillation from one potential career to another.

"At Christmas my younger sister, who had already received two advanced degrees, insisted that we spend some time together. I shall never forget the conversation we had over lunch. She pinned me down by asking some rather direct questions. 'If you had no limitations, what would you do?'

"At the time I thought she was just being a nosy sister,

but I soon realized that she had deeper insights into my lack of fulfillment than I had.

" 'What's missing, Teresa?' she asked.

"I stumbled for an answer. 'My babies are growing up. They don't need me like they have in the past. My three kids are my identity. Now that they are establishing their own lives and identities, I feel I am losing mine.'

"I suddenly realized what I had said. If my good and my identity is only woven tightly to my kids, I am setting myself up for pain. The moment will come when children will be grown, then what? I guess you could say I had an extreme case of empty nest phobia.

"Regardless of my reasons for not making a change, my sister continued to press for an answer. 'What would you do if you could do anything?'

"I couldn't answer her. Instead of solutions, all I could see were my limitations and obvious obstacles. I had a family. I had church responsibilities. My list seemed infinite.

"It was then that she turned the paper place mat over and drew two vertical lines. In the left column she wrote *Dreams*. In the right column she wrote *Limitations*. And in the center column she wrote *Solutions*.

	Dreams	Solutions	Limitations
1.			
2.			
3.			

"She then asked me to identify my number one dream. My thinking had been locked in neutral for so long I had to struggle to get it in gear. Finally, I said it. College. I wanted to go back to college and finish my degree.

" 'Great,' she said. 'Write that in the left-hand column. Now, what is keeping you from doing that?' she asked.

"The answers were endless. Who will take care of my children? Who will run errands for my husband? I have so many responsibilities connected to my family and church. I am a room mother, an officer at PTA, our church's missions education leader for girls. The list seemed infinite. Besides, I have been out of school for over 12 years. What if I fail! Ouch!"

" 'Enough,' she said. 'Let's now write at least three solutions for each of your obstacles.' It was then that I realized that it could be done. With a little hesitation, I announced: 'I'm going back to college. I may only take one course at a time, but I'm going! And tomorrow I'm going to take the first step. I will get an application and catalogue.'

"After college I pursued a career in education. Teaching and working with children was not a new experience for me. I had been teaching my kids for years prior to entering school. But juggling my new career, husband, children, and church responsibilities was a skill that was not taught in school. At times I had to drop one ball in order to catch the other. The key, I feel, is balance.

"But trying to balance the many dimensions of life has its drawbacks. Regardless of how much support and family cooperation you receive, it is emotionally stressful. It's still hard for me to leave my children each morning. In fact, I mentally take them with me most of my 20-mile drive to school. And often I find myself trying to fit my 165 students into my small car at the end of the day.

"Juggling has it advantages too. I find that my time with my family is more intense and of better quality. I feel that I appreciate and savor every moment with them. My relationship with Milt is better than ever before. Our admiration for one another continues to grow. He seems proud of me for taking on what seemed to be an impossible challenge. I admire him for the many ways he has juggled his schedule to help around the house. As far as the kids, I sense they are more responsible than before. And because I work with children every day, I feel I am more in touch with them.

"To sum it up, my life is really no different than before. There is just more of it!"

As I drove back to Birmingham after what I felt was an exhilarating interview, I could not help dwelling on her last closing comment. "My life is really no different than before. There is just more of it!" I left Teresa feeling 100 percent confident that she had achieved "more of it." But how? Could it be that sincerity, conviction, purpose, and a deep commitment to Christ had motivated her to extend herself beyond what even she may once have insisted were her human limitations? And while I knew firsthand that Teresa's Christian witness illuminated the many lives that she touched each day, I still wondered how she did it. Evidently, I was not the only one who wondered what the driving force was behind Teresa and the hundreds of thousands of working mothers whose lives are evidence of a trend which is rapidly sweeping across our country—a trend that will not likely reverse.

As I studied Teresa's life, I could not help applauding her accomplishments. Yet, I still wondered. Is her life typical? She seems almost too good to be true. Because I am not married and live alone, I can avoid comparing my life with hers. But it is fun to imagine what my life would be like given the same set of circumstances. I doubt I would be described as a Miss America look-alike who has it all and can do it all. Instead I feel quite confident that I would join the majority of women who struggle, have warts, are less-than-perfect, and who are forced to constantly deal with some amount of mediocrity.

While I cannot help but affirm that Teresa is extremely gifted and outstanding, I likewise cannot help but wonder if being outstanding is the same as being super.

As women enter the work force at an unprecedented rate, a rate which is predicted to increase to 60 percent by the end of the century, I can't help feeling that women have been victimized by a media myth which insists that super-mom is the star.[2] From the covers of countless women's magazines displayed at the grocery checkout counter leaps "today's woman"—neatly dressed in a gray or blue "power suit" with matching pumps; a briefcase strapped to one shoulder; a bag of nutritious groceries embraced in one arm while a healthy, happy baby bounces on the other hip. She is the prototype of having it all, being all, and doing all.

Am I the only one that wonders what a mother has to give up in order to be super? What is a supermom anyway? Will these supermoms continue to juggle it all? Will they go out of fashion? Or will they just plain wear out?

Experts who focus on women's roles are gravitating toward a point of neutrality—that is, working will continue to be "in" for women; however, the scores of women who continue to juggle multifaceted roles are either wearing out or renovating their life's priorities.

Lili Sikorski-Smith, a clinical psychologist whose primary practice focuses on women, explains, "When women moved into the work force and into achieved roles, they did not let go of their ascribed roles. First of all, they found that 'no one is satisfactorily assuming their responsibilities within the home. Rarely was anyone on the job supportive of special needs they have had by being wives, mothers, and employees.' "[3]

After reading Sikorski-Smith's comments, I felt compelled to probe even deeper. The perfect candidate for this interview, I felt, was my friend and former co-worker, Melinda. Like Teresa, Melinda was a woman who represented having done it all, but in a different order.

I called Melinda earlier in the day hoping that she could make arrangements with her husband, Walter, to keep their two preschoolers while we met. We were in luck. Walter would be home by 6:00 P.M. I picked up Melinda at 6:30. After hugs and last-minute instructions regarding her children's dinner, Melinda and I were off to a quiet restaurant. Over coffee I confessed:

"The day you told me that you had decided to resign in order to stay home with your children remains on my list of very bad days. As editor and consultant, we were a team. Our work simply clicked. Why did you hold out so long?

What was your reason for trying to do it all?"

Melinda's answer was simple, yet profound. "To not do it all meant either giving up my career, my marriage, or neglecting my kids. Like other working women I know, I found myself in a constant state of motion as I continually reacted to the needs of others. It was a myth for me to believe that I could totally break away from the home front in order to embrace a career and all life's opportunities and options that were before me, opportunities that my mother and grandmother never had. But in reality I never let go of the home front at all.

"Likewise, it was a myth for me to believe that I could manage a career, two children under age three, my home, and church responsibilities as well. I shall never forget the pressure. It was not uncommon for me to start my day at 4:00 A.M. in order to wash clothes and clean the house before starting breakfast and preparing myself for work. And there were those dreadful nights when my job responsibilities demanded that I work late.

"Even when I had made arrangements for proper child care, I often felt like a taxi with the meter running. I finally realized I was literally paying a baby-sitter in order for me to work. As for Walter, I guess we got tired of communicating with notes taped on the refrigerator door and trying to define exactly what constitutes quality time."

Melinda is not alone in her dilemma. She joins the ranks of others who are asking themselves, Do I want to bake my bread, shop for it, or eat out?

"Melinda," I asked. "From your experience as a wife and mother who juggled a career, what would you identify as key issues affecting women who work?"

"Perhaps the first thing I should say is working for a paycheck versus working without a paycheck is an emotionally charged issue for mothers. Until I had a baby, I had no concept of all the issues surrounding finding and keeping child care. Not only is child care an emotional issue, it is an economic issue and employment issue as well. Another issue affecting the quality of life for employed mothers is the absence or presence of a support system. In our case, we didn't have one.

"I readily admit I had days when I wish I could be back at work—those days when my agenda at home turns into confetti. Those are the days when a child lets the dog out into the neighborhood and I have to play dogcatcher instead of buying groceries; the days when someone is constantly crying, snatching, pushing, tattling, spilling something, breaking something, throwing up, or any of a number of other things that aren't too pleasant. They're not being bad; they're just being kids.

"On days like that, I tend to crave the tranquility and civility of the office, where life was a lot more predictable than it is now and people were a lot more affirming and I could see more measurable results from my efforts. But I also know that my children are going to have those strange days even if I am at an office somewhere. And I'd much rather they be surrounded on those days by someone who loves them and is willing to teach them to respond appropriately than by someone for whom caring for their physical needs is just a job.

"For women living in the trenches of ordinary "momdom," "supermomdom" is a hot issue. As for me, I don't want to be called a supermom. Instead, I want to be a good mom in the sight of God and my children."

For Melinda, quitting work did not mean losing a career. Instead, it meant postponing it. Likewise, for Teresa going to work did not mean abandoning her family. Instead, it meant expanding it.

As I examined the lives of Teresa and Melinda, I began to realize that I would do well if I switched my focus from what they did to who they are. Both women, Teresa and Melinda, live lives which demonstrate a consistent, similar purpose—to make a difference in their world for Jesus

Christ. I have spent hours watching both women at work and at play. Likewise, I have observed firsthand as both women of faith live out their faith and exhibit a Christian witness where they are—at work, at the market, and at home. Instead of desiring to be a supermom, they desire to be a good mom in the sight of God. They want no part in the guilt producing "supermomdom" which may be to the 1990s what keeping up with the Joneses was to the 1950s and 1960s.

Getting INtouch

Why is it so difficult to combine both job and family? After all, isn't autonomy and a clear sense of identity what women have wanted for years? Twenty years ago thousands of women stormed the streets in nearly every major city in an effort to declare themselves able to oversee their own destinies. What went wrong? Why are so many working women now claiming that they feel estranged, fragmented, and torn apart?

Perhaps the good news is that the bad news is wrong. After interviewing several Christian women who struggle to balance the many dimensions of their lives, I learned not only what the struggle was but what it was not. The struggle is not schedules nor the difficulty regarding who goes where when. The struggle is not about household responsibilities or even child care, although these are struggles worthy of being called major concerns.

No, the struggle is about identity. Lodged deep within the women I interviewed raged the battle of identity. The battle for who we are may well have an impact on every aspect of the lives of hundreds of thousands of women.

And hidden even deeper, often disguised, is insistently erupting a painful emotion: guilt. The litany of guilt rings across the country as women cry, "I feel guilty about everything. Then I feel guilty about feeling guilty." This nagging guilt favors no one—not even the single mother who must work in order to provide food for her children. Where does this guilt come from? Is it the legacy of domesticity? Can women who hold jobs escape from this plague?

Please note that the motivational factor urging most women to return to work was not self-actualization or even personal fulfillment as might be expected. Instead it was a response to simple home economics. In a survey conducted by *Working Mother* magazine 95 percent of the women who responded—whether blue-collar or white-collar, older or younger—indicated that their main reason for working was the money. But when asked if they would quit their jobs if they could afford to, only 15 percent of the respondents said that they would.

Regardless of how you divide it, a day still consists of 24 hours. Women who choose to work and try to have it all must also choose what they will give up. In reality no one has it all. Women who work outside the home do gain an income, a sense of accomplishment, a sense of independence, as well as the opportunity to meet new people with shared interests; but those same women miss a great deal too.

As a working woman who is single and without children, I feel ill prepared to suggest from where the guilt might come. Perhaps guilt is the result of feeling that our life's choices are exclusive rather than inclusive.

However, I do wonder what I might have done had my life's choices been different. Had I married a handsome prince and had children, would I have continued my profession? Would I have worked until the children were born, or joined the ranks of those women whose home telephone number is their work number as well? I must confess, I am uncomfortable with these questions. May I submit to you that we might be asking the wrong questions? Instead of focusing on the conflicts resulting from all of the shoulds and oughts that make us try to be all things to all people at all times, could it be that our focus and attention should be replaced as we concentrate on our purpose in life? And as we identify our purpose through concentrated prayer and Bible study, do we not also identify our priorities? Could it be that what is a priority in my life may not be a priority in my friend's life?

I know that some women may feel more comfortable with a general pattern of living for all women; in other words, what's right for one woman is right for all. But, personally, I am not comfortable making such broad and general assumptions. For just as each woman's fingerprint is unique, so is her family situation, economic status, and calling in life. And since I can find nowhere in God's Word that gives me the authority to force my values on my friends, I am convinced that I must shun the temptation to judge.

Getting Involved

If it is not my responsibility to judge the lives of others and to set the record straight, what is my responsibility? Once again I submit to you, women of faith, that our responsibilities go deeper. We must not close our eyes and pretend that all is well on the home front when we see children left for hours without parental support. Likewise, we cannot assume that just because a woman works outside the home her family and spiritual life have gone down the drain. As women of faith, I encourage you not only to recognize the problems that do arise for some women as they move into the work force but to contribute to the answers as well.

First, we do well to realize that the trend discussed in this chapter isn't likely to reverse, at least not in this decade. And, regardless of our position, what matters most is our concern and support of women we know who are sitting behind the desk or standing in front of the kitchen stove. We must depart from the temptation to declare what is best for her and her family; and, in the empty space where criticism may have resided, put our concern and support. When we see our friends struggle to fulfill what they have identified as God's purpose in their lives, may we, women of faith, be there for them both ready and willing to encourage and nurture in Jesus' name.

How will you touch the lives of those women who are trying to do all and be all? In the space below, write the name of a woman you know who struggles to juggle it all. (While any one of us could write our own name in the space below, it is critical that we reach outside ourselves.)

List at least three actions you can put to work right away to relieve some of the stress and strain in her life. Your answer could include providing child care or volunteering services (grocery shopping, mending clothes, doing laundry).

In what way can these actions become an entry point in sharing Christ's love?

[1]David E. Bloom, "Women and Work," *American Demographics* (September 1986): 26.
[2]Ibid., 30.
[3]Diane Mason, "Superwoman's Fall from Role Model to Syndrome," *St. Petersburg Times*, February 16, 1986. Reprinted from *Women*, vol. 3 (Boca Raton, FL: Social Issues Resources Series, 1989), Article no. 43.

6

Caught in the Middle

Learn first of all to put [your] religion into practice by caring for [your] own family and so repaying [your] parents and grandparents, for this is pleasing to God.

1 Timothy 5:4 (NIV)
(author's paraphrase)

The shrill ringing of the telephone caused me to bolt up in bed. I glanced at the clock radio on the small night table next to my bed. It was 6:15 A.M. Who could possibly be calling at this early hour on Saturday morning? I wondered. I quickly threw back the warm blanket and sprang to my feet. I staggered to the telephone located in the hallway.

"Hello."

"Marsha, it's Georgia. I hope I didn't awaken you."

"I needed to get up. Are we still meeting for breakfast?"

"That's why I am calling. This is not a good day. Mother fell again last night. I feel sure her hip is broken. The baby is screaming and Bernie is demanding my complete attention as usual. I feel my entire life is being sabotaged by someone or something totally outside my control."

I could tell from Georgia's voice that she was near her breaking point. She had called on many occasions when she needed someone to simply listen, but the tension in her voice was different this morning. I felt a tingling sensation of concern. All that was within me wanted to reach out and embrace her pain. Yet I realized that other than being an encouraging and supporting friend who listened with genu-

69

ine concern, there was little I could do.

"Georgia, where is Karen? Could she take care of Bernie and her baby while you take your mother to the hospital?"

"Not a chance. I haven't seen Karen in two or three days. I don't even know where she is. She only shows up when she is hungry, needs a place to sleep, or needs money. Even if she were here, I wouldn't trust her alone with the baby and Bernie."

"Listen, I can be there in about 15 minutes. Would you either let me stay with Bernie and Melissa or let me take your mother to the emergency room? You know you will at least need help getting your mother in the car."

Georgia's voice quivered as she quietly accepted my offer.

"Sit tight, friend. I am on my way."

As I dressed, my heart grieved for Georgia. If ever there was a giving and compassionate lady, it was Georgia Kennedy. But the cold, hard realities of life had settled under her roof. Georgia was the main caregiver for her disabled husband in his late 60s. Bernie's paralysis was a result of a massive stroke only three years ago. Even though he is completely paralyzed on his right side, he is still a lucky man. At the time of his stroke Georgia was told by his physician that he had less than a 1 percent chance to live. Bernie's partial recovery was simply miraculous.

You would think that Bernie would be grateful for life. Yet that is far from the truth. Before his illness, Bernie had been one of his church's most active members. Unlike many who choose to grow from their pain, Bernie has chosen the path of bitterness. The change in him was first noticed after he was released from the rehabilitation hospital. He refused to receive visitors and often refused even to open one of the hundreds of get-well cards sent from concerned friends.

As the weeks grew into months, Bernie began to alienate himself from everyone except Georgia. My observation is that Georgia has become his servant. Bernie's doctors have explained to Georgia that some of Bernie's personality disorder could be due to the stroke. Regardless, Bernie is not

70

the only one to suffer. Georgia's life is really no life at all. The demands placed on Georgia seem to be impossible to fulfill.

What's worse is that Bernie doesn't seem to notice that there is anyone else living at the Kennedy residence with needs to be filled. Mrs. Thompson, Georgia's 89-year-old mother, is an example. After Georgia's father died, Mrs. Thompson moved in with Georgia and Bernie.

To others it might seem that Mrs. Thompson could be a comfort and support for Georgia. Wrong again. Not unlike Bernie, Mrs. Thompson has her own demanding agenda. I can remember Georgia commenting once that her mother was as strong as an ox and as mean as a snake. Not only does she wander around the house half the night, but it is not uncommon to find her wandering around in the neighborhood at 1:00 A.M.

Old age itself is part of Mrs. Thompson's problem. Seldom does she remember to turn off the stove. She snaps at Bernie and becomes extremely agitated when baby Melissa cries. Bernie, in turn, takes his frustration regarding his live-in mother-in-law out on Georgia—the only moving target strong enough to withstand his verbal and emotional abuse. Seldom does a week go by that Bernie doesn't threaten to kick his aging mother-in-law out of the house. Frankly, nothing would please him more since such an arrangement would put Georgia in a position to focus even more of her undivided attention on him. With the exception of brief visits with friends over the telephone, Georgia has little contact with the outside world.

I grieve for Georgia, but my grief and concern grow deeper when I think about Melissa, Georgia's 15-month-old granddaughter. Georgia's only child, Karen, got pregnant before her 17th birthday. No one really knows who the father is, not even Karen. But that's not the worst of it. Unfortunately, while Karen was carrying Melissa, she was on crack (a highly concentrated derivative of cocaine). To Georgia, Karen was the only teenaged girl in the world whose life has erupted into a complete mess. Unfortunately, Georgia is not alone as a mother grieving about her daughter's rebellious and irresponsible behavior. In spite of the Christian values that Georgia tried so hard to inscribe in her daughter's heart, Karen is one of millions who have made choices that resulted in catastrophe.

As I drove to Georgia's house, my mind continued to race forward with thoughts about Karen and her baby. If only Karen could admit her drug problem. But, as is typical of drug abusers, she denies her insidious habit. Karen's denial goes deeper than her illegal drug problem. Karen assumes absolutely no responsibility for Melissa—her 15-month-old "crack" baby (one whose mother did crack during the first trimester of pregnancy).

I remember the first day I saw Melissa. She couldn't have been more than 30 minutes old. At that time none of us knew she was a crack baby. Melissa was beautiful. And while Georgia knew that this tiny one would ultimately become another responsibility for her, there was something special about this new life. While the circumstances regarding Melissa's birth were painful, there was a fresh joy that comes when an innocent little person enters your life.

Melissa was only 2 hours old when Georgia's ray of sunshine became cloudy. The hospital's resident pediatrician asked to speak to Georgia privately in one of the family consultation rooms. It was there that Georgia learned of Melissa's problems. Melissa was a "blue baby." Testing revealed a critical heart defect. When Melissa was only 2 days old, she underwent open-heart surgery.

Even though she survived surgery, the worst was far from over. Melissa's doctor was unaware that Karen had been on crack. While still in the surgical recovery room, little Melissa began to have seizures, a common result of sudden withdrawal from a hard narcotic, cocaine, or crack.

Further testing indicated brain damage. For 6 weeks Melissa was cared for in the hospital's detoxification unit. During these weeks Georgia was told by Melissa's physician that

72

she was ceasing to thrive. Melissa needed to bond with her mother, but by this time Karen was nowhere to be found. And so the story goes. Georgia was caught in the middle.

Since Georgia was unable to leave Bernie and her mother for any length of time, church members volunteered to spend up to 8 hours a day simply holding and feeding little Melissa. Without human touch, Melissa would have died.

Moments before arriving at Georgia's house a stunning thought echoed inside my head. Was Georgia's situation unique? How many women in their 50s and 60s are actually caught in the middle with family tension and responsibilities pulling from both sides? If the pull is strong enough, could Georgia be torn in two? It's true. I could instantly think of at least a half a dozen couples whose adult children had now moved back home for various reasons. And with the outrageous cost of health care for the elderly, how many men and women Georgia's age are experiencing a parental inversion whereby they assume responsibility for their parents?

As I walked up the sidewalk toward Georgia's house, I made a commitment to explore more deeply my thoughts and questions. What I found was a painful trend. What I do with what I know can greatly affect the lives of all the Georgias in my life who are literally caught in the middle.

Getting INtouch

In the 1980s life belonged to the young. As the 1990s usher in the twenty-first century, life belongs to the old, since over 25 percent of the American population will be aged 65 and older. This number is expected to double in the next few decades. By 2050, the number of Americans 80 and above could reach 25 million. The old will, therefore, become the fastest growing segment of the American population. It is estimated that elderly women will outnumber men 3 to 2. As the elderly segment of our population increases, so will the number of three-generation families in which the children, parents, and grandparents share living space and responsibilities.

To many the three-generation family is a trend unique to the 1990s. However, such a view is a myth. Moving in with the folks—or moving in with the kids—was an economical necessity as much as four decades ago. Only in the last couple of decades have families become independent due to urbanization and mobilization.

By probing deeply one can see that the life-style of the 1990s may be slowly reverting toward life-styles of 40 years ago. Research reveals that 3.5 million elderly (12.2 percent) have incomes below the poverty level. And 20 percent of all elderly widows are considered poor. The United States has the third largest elderly population (age 65 +) and the largest "old-old" population (80 +) in the world. The poverty rate among the elderly in the United States is soaring.

In addition to the economic crunch that attacks the elderly, 1 of 4 elderly have at least a mild degree of functional disability, while a full 50 percent of the oldest old have some functional disability. Those with functional limitations include

difficulty in walking: 18.7 percent
getting outside: 9.6 percent
getting in or out of bed or chair: 8 percent
preparing meals: 7 percent
shopping for personal items: 11.3 percent
managing money: 5 percent
using the telephone: 5 percent
doing heavy housework: 24 percent
doing light housework: 7 percent

Recent studies reveal that older adults have a higher suicide rate than any other age group.

As the number of aged increases, so does the need for caregivers. In 1982 relatives represented 84 percent of all caregivers and provided 89 percent of all days of care for disabled members in their family. An incredibly high number of Americans between ages 40 and 60 are the primary caregivers for their ailing or frail parents as well as other relatives. Astonishing statistics released from the American Association of Retired Persons (AARP) show that there are approximately 7 million Georgias out there; 3 out of 4 are women, and half hold down a job outside the home.

More specifically, "disabled elderly are three times more likely to be cared for by adult daughters than to be institutionalized. Daughters (29 percent) are the primary caregivers of elderly followed by wives (23 percent), husbands (13 percent), and 'formal services' (10 percent). The remaining 25 percent includes neighbors, other relatives, nonprofessionals, nonrelatives, and others."[1]

A special report released by the National Center for Health Statistics revealed that "12 percent of the adult daughters had to quit work to care for these disabled elderly." To complicate the home front, over 40 percent of these women are still raising their own families and are truly caught in the middle.

According to Joan Kuriansky, executive director of the Older Women's League, an organization that has done a great deal to publicize the caregivers' situation, "These caregivers are society's heroes. They do double and triple duty to keep relatives out of institutions."[2]

AARP research reveals that over 90 percent of ill older people live in their own homes or with family members who can provide all their care.

At least 80 percent of all caregivers are on call seven days a week. Chores include personal care and hygiene, dressing, household errands, transportation, cooking, grocery shopping, household finances, and administering medication for their frail aging loved ones. In addition, the majority of these caregivers are also caring for their own children and households.

Caregivers like Georgia perform their duties without recognition, much less rest. But what is often not realized is that the constant pressure of being caught in the middle can be detrimental to the physical and psychological health of the caregiver.

Why does the burden fall on the family of the aging? The answer varies, but common threads seem to be obvious in nearly every caretaker's situation. All too often aging caretakers wait for a crisis before seeking relief from their burdensome responsibilities. Other family, therefore, may be the only ones they can call. In addition, love for the relative, an uncomfortable feeling about having strangers caring for their ailing loved one, a sense of duty, and not knowing where to find service may make the caretaker feel she must do everything herself.

But the facts seem clear that the caretaker needs all the help and support she can get. Notice I said "she," since the majority of caretakers are women. Even small amounts of relief in the form of support or help go a long way and may well mean the difference between coping and crisis. Such help can come from home health workers who donate a few hours a day.

While being the primary caretaker for aging parents is itself an emotional and physical burden, caring for the old is only one source of pressure confronting middle-aged women today. Pressure also comes from adult children still dependent on their parents financially, emotionally, and for room and board.

Caring for Mom and Dad is made more difficult by having adult children move home. When these children bring their children into the home, the pressure can be unbearable on the caregiver.

What is evident is that the immediate family of the older person is by far the major source of support in time of illness or crisis. This is such a social expectation that we should see parent care as a normal family stress. It becomes clear that not only do adult children not thoughtlessly dump their parents into nursing homes, they usually go to the end of their rope and beyond before turning to institutional care as a last resort.

Let me underscore that feeling an obligation to care for Mom or Dad is nothing new. What is new is the great number of the very old and the emerging phenomenon of a meaningful number of dependent people who have now survived into their late 80s and 90s. The caretakers of an 89-year-old may themselves be senior adults. Feelings of burden not only are common but also are related to how dependent the older relative is and how much help is provided by other family members.

The caregiver who is all alone is the one most likely to run out of gas. As women of faith in the 1990s, we must take note. In an age of rising divorce rates and declining birth rates we will see an increasingly aging group of people who have fewer and fewer available caretakers. If the burden of dependency falls on just one individual, resentment can lead to abuse. Dependency is the principal correlate of elder abuse, and the person who has no help and who is running short on resources is the most likely to abuse. Christian women, we must get involved.

Getting Involved

It takes time and ingenuity to discover ways to minister to those who are juggling the many responsibilities of being a caregiver. But with patience, true friends, and the help of organizations whose primary concern is the elderly, help is available.

First, become familiar with the types of assistance now available and begin to discuss these options long before a crisis occurs. Below are a samples of services available in most communities.

In-home service: When minimal help is all that is needed to keep an elderly person independent, home-delivery programs, such as Meals on Wheels, are a practical solution. These types of programs are among the most frequently used community resource for homebound people. The Meals on Wheels program delivers nutritious lunches and dinners to the door on a weekly basis. Such services can help prevent unhealthy eating habits, save money, and provide the elderly with regular and predictable social contact.

Telephone reassurance programs: Volunteers call the elderly two or three times a week to combat isolation. Paging services (found in the yellow pages) also provide a sense of security for frail elderly persons.

Community escort services: For those who have trouble getting around, these services provide transportation to and from doctor appointments and other activities.

Day workers: These workers are available for hire for those who require companions to accompany them on walks or errands. Such home health care includes housekeeping, preparing meals, dressing, and limited personal care. Visiting nurse services may also be available for those who require the services of a registered nurse.

Respite service: According to Avalie Saperstein, director of social services at the Philadelphia Geriatric Center, many caregivers don't go on vacation. Respite services relieve mental stress and help them cope better with caregiving. One form of respite is found in the more than 2,000 adult day-care centers now in the United States. Some are mainly social centers. Others also offer health care such as physical, occupational, or speech therapy; as well as appointments with health professionals.

Although the elderly person may not want to go to the center at first, experienced caregivers suggest a trial period of a few weeks. Often the person needs only a little time to adjust.

Churches: Many churches maintain a referral list of persons willing to work an occasional day, weekend, or week to give the caregiver some time off. Some nursing homes around the country are now offering short-term admissions, usually for a minimum of two weeks, for the same purpose.

Private geriatric care managers: This is something new in services for the elderly. Such care management is provided on a fee basis by an increasing number of professionals in response to public need. This resource is particularly useful for caregivers living a long distance from their parents. For information on care managers in your area, contact the National Association of Private Geriatric Care Managers, 1315 Talbott Tower, Dayton, OH 45402; phone (513) 222-2621.

Special housing assistance: For those who don't need 24-hour care, but do need special housing assistance, new housing options are available. For example, independent-living centers offer services such as home-delivered meals and emergency response systems to those able to take care of themselves.

Nursing homes: A nursing home may be the best place for those elderly persons who have Alzheimer's disease or some other serious medical condition to receive care. Although the elderly person loses independence, he or she benefits from 24-hour medical supervision. Nursing homes also provide opportunities to meet other people and participate in a variety of activities. Families should begin considering a nursing home while the elderly person is still able to take part in the decision. It is possible to locate a very good nursing home because of the close supervision by state regulatory agencies.

Support groups: These groups are advantageous to both the caregiver and the one receiving care. The caregiver can meet regularly with others in similar situations and learn about local services and practical coping skills. The caregiver is reminded to look after her own welfare also.

Education: Classes on caring for older parents are provided by many hospitals and social service agencies. Classes provide information on how to cope with their aging parents.

Additional information about local services is available from a variety of sources.

Ask your family doctor for information about support services in your community.

Contact state and local agencies on aging. Check under

Aging or Senior Citizens or Social Services in the government listing or yellow pages in your telephone book.

Many hospitals now have geriatric evaluation centers staffed by medical and social service workers. Such services can evaluate the needs of frail individuals and their caregivers. They can also make referrals to community services.

Family Services America, a nonprofit organization with 290 members, can provide services to and/or make referrals to other community resources for elderly persons and their families. For more information, send a self-addressed stamped envelope to Family Services America, 11700 West Lake Park Drive, Milwaukee, WI 53224; or call (414) 359-2111.

Contact your church and its related social service agencies.

For information on caregiver support groups near you, write the National Council on Aging, 600 Maryland Avenue, SW, West Wing 100, Washington, DC 20024; or call (202) 479-1200.

The report "Caregivers of the Frail Elderly: A National Profile" can be secured by sending a self-addressed, self-adhesive mailing label to NCHRS Publications and Information Branch, 1-46 Part Building, Rockville, MD 20857.[3]

Who do you know that is caught in the middle? Write their names below.

What can you do to relieve at least one pressure that is squeezing in on their lives?

---

[1]Marilynn Kelly, ed., "RD Digest," vol. 8, no. 8 (Atlanta: Home Mission Board, September 1986): 4.

[2]Ronni Sandroff, "Caught in the Middle: Caring for Your Aging Parents and Your Children," *Health Report* (Knoxville, TN: Whittle Communications L. P., 1989).

[3]Ibid.

7

Combating Violence

Rescue me, O Lord, from evil men; protect me from men of violence, who devise evil plans in their hearts. . . . Keep me, O Lord, from the hands of the wicked.
Psalm 140:1-4 (NIV)

Janice's voice quivered as she tried to explain why she had come to the emergency shelter.

"We had only been married three weeks when it started. He hit me so hard I fell to the floor. I was so frightened; I had never seen Jerry like that before. He was upset because I had gone next door to have coffee with Renee without telling him first. That's when he locked me in the hall closet for two days. But after he let me out, he said he was sorry.

"His attacks have gotten progressively worse. In the six years that we have been married I have been slapped across the face, tied to the kitchen table. He has even threatened to kill me if I failed to obey. I don't know if I can stand it anymore. I'm so afraid of him; but I still love him. I promised to stand by him for better or worse. Does that mean I have to stay with my husband until he kills me?"

While Janice's story is one filled with terror, Janice is still one of the luckier ones. Because Renee suspected that Janice was being battered, she courageously contacted the authorities. As a result of Renee's support, Janice sought refuge at a community emergency shelter. Unlike many victims of domestic crimes, Janice is alive today.

Susan Fletcher was not so lucky. After years of abuse, Susan Fletcher did everything the courts asked. She moved away from her husband, Bruce; got an unlisted telephone number; and got an order of protection warning him to stay away.

"He told me he was going to beat me and take my kids from me, so that I would never see them again; and that he would make my life so miserable that I would wish daily that I was dead," she once said.

While out on an eight-hour prison pass, Bruce found Susan and beat her to death outside her home in Kentucky.

Like Susan, Carol Jackson looked to the system for protection. She even called the 911 number in her city to warn the police that her husband was on his way to kill her. All calls received from a 911 number are recorded. On November 6, 1989, NBC's "The Today Show" played the recording.

"He hasn't come over yet but he is threatening to do so. I am sure he will."

"Well, what you need to do is call us if he comes over there. You see, we can't have a unit sit there and wait to see if he comes over there."

"Oh no, please help."

When the police did arrive, Carol and two others were dead.

Unfortunately, Susan and Carol were unable to get help in their most desperate time of need. The result of not having a backup support system proved to be deadly. Fortunately, not all women who are victims of domestic violence live in constant fear. There is hope available for women who know where to turn. In Waco, Texas, hope for the battered and abused is available because of Frances (Fran) Booth Porter.

Since January 1988 Fran has been director of Sanctuary Home, a transitional housing program for abused women and children in the Waco area. The shelter opened with only one resident, a 65-year-old woman who not only had been married 35 years but had likewise been abused 35 years. The woman was found by Waco police, who discovered her sleeping in a parked car. When the authorities insisted that she go home because it was not safe for her to sleep in a car, she replied, "I can't go home; it's not safe there."

If we could follow Fran throughout a typical day, we might find her juggling roles as a mother, fund-raiser, counselor, chauffeur, and apartment manager. When Fran is not responding to crisis or special needs through listening and encouraging, she can be found sitting at her desk with a child in her lap.

Fran's goal is to provide a safe place for women and children who are victims of abuse. The program not only provides a place of refuge, it also allows women time to search the job market and develop vocational skills. Medical services and on-site counseling are also made available at the Sanctuary Home.

"While not a religious institution per se, the home seeks to be a nurturing Christian environment and church attendance is encouraged. . . .

"Sensitive church members who are 'in tune' with the persons in their missions group or Sunday School class know when a person is going through something. Perhaps they can't identify the problem, but they can let people know they are available. Ministry doesn't mean prying, delving, taking sides. . . . Our job is not to give permission or condone or even totally understand a problem but to accept what a person is going through," said Fran.[1]

The question for women of faith may be Are we willing to admit that domestic violence is real and that the victim could be sitting next to us in church Sunday morning?

Getting INtouch

Nothing denotes warmth, love, and security more than the home. Historically, the home has been considered the nucleus of society. As children we found safety and security from the dangers of our world at home. But in reality few places are as violent as the home.

Our society gives much attention to public violence, making us feel vulnerable outside our own home. Excluding the military and police, the family is our nation's most violent social group.

A person is more likely to be a victim of violence at home than any other place, with the attacker being a family member rather than a stranger. Unfortunately, an inescapable fact prevails: People are being victimized in epidemic numbers at home by those closest to them. And the devastating impact of domestic violence touches every one of us. Studies suggest that "90 percent of incarcerated violent offenders were themselves victims of violent homes."[2]

Violence against women is a domestic crime of enormous proportion. Some experts feel that domestic violence is as common as love. Each year millions of women receive medical attention for injuries that are believed to have occurred as a result of being beaten by their husbands or boyfriends. Because victims are fearful, ashamed, or indifferent, many crimes are not reported; so it is difficult to estimate exactly how many women are abused each year.

Likewise, it has been only in recent years that statistics have been collected in a systematic way by authorities.

Most recently, the Federal Bureau of Investigation (FBI) estimates that 1 out of 2 women will be physically abused by a man with whom she lives at some point in her life. In any given year approximately 6,000,000 wives (legal or common law) are abused by their husbands. Every year 2,000 to 4,000 women are beaten to death.

Furthermore, the FBI claims that during one year alone 40 percent of the women killed in America were murdered by their husbands.[3] That translates into more than 4 women being killed by their intimate partners *every day* in America.

In an effort to put the raw data into perspective, realize that "roughly every other married woman you meet will at some point in her marriage experience at least one incident of physical violence at the hands of her husband."[4]

Because of the nature of violence and evil, no one is

exempt from being abused—Christian, atheist, pauper, or millionaire can be abusers or abused. It is no respecter of persons. An abused wife may live in a shabby apartment, a new condominium, a little mobile home, or a three-story house. She may be your next-door neighbor or even share your church pew.

Unfortunately, women are not the only victims of abuse. "The number of child abuse cases is conservatively estimated at well over 1,000,000 a year, with experts stating that this figure represents only 10 to 20 percent of the actual number of cases. About 5 percent of dependent elderly Americans are physically abused within their own home by relatives, their children or grandchildren."[5]

Just as the victims of domestic violence may come from virtually any walk of life, so do the abusers. The battering husband may be anyone, including a well-respected church leader or a close personal friend. Because they are good at hiding their abusive nature, few outsiders suspect what they are like. All too often, when an abused wife comes forward, her story is not believed by friends and other family members.

While it is often thought that abuse only takes place in homes where the husband is an alcoholic or where couples are only nominal Christians, we must recognize that chemical substance abuse is not necessarily to be blamed for a man's violence against his wife. Drinking does lower a person's control and inhibitions, but drinking is not the root of the problem. Furthermore, contrary to popular belief, most batterers are not considered to be psychotics. In fact, the majority lead normal lives. The root of their problem stems from the inability to deal with frustration and anger.

Many were abused as children. Because they are insecure, they need to live up to a tough-guy image.

"Statistics gathered nationwide indicate that the highest rates of violence are found among families without religious affiliation, and in families where the husband is unemployed."[6] While there are few studies to accurately suggest

85

just how common domestic violence is in the Christian home, one report does confirm that more nonreligious than religious homes are involved in expressions of violence.

It is interesting to note that while violence levels were not appreciably different for families from various religious groups, violence levels were noted to be high for families in which the spouses' denominational commitment differed. So don't assume that religious beliefs will prevent battering. While one study cannot be considered as an authoritative analysis of the problem in Christian homes, "one can conservatively estimate that for every 60 married women in a church, 10 suffer emotional and verbal abuse, and 2 or 3 will be physically abused by their husbands."[7]

As a Christian woman, I have found confronting the problem of domestic abuse to be as complex, frightening, and frustrating as any issue impacting the lives of women. Just what constitutes abuse? Does it apply to a woman who is slapped once by her husband? Some women verbally assault their husbands until a fight breaks out. And some women may never receive a single blow, but repeated emotional abuse will destroy all sense of self-worth. Are all of these greater or lesser degrees of wife abuse? Unfortunately, the answer is a haunting yes.

Domestic abuse may come in any number and variety of forms. Psychological and verbal abuse is most common. Such abuse deteriorates the self-esteem of the victim. Verbal accusations, extreme suspicion or jealousy, and terrorism with threats of death to the wife and children are not uncommon. Although nonphysical abuse (such as humiliation and harassment) can be terribly painful, it is not likely to be life threatening unless the individual being abused has a propensity toward suicide. Physical abuse is yet another thing; it can easily become a matter of life and death. Physical abuse can be pushing, slapping, hitting, kicking, choking, biting, burning, hair pulling, and using weapons.

Perhaps you are wondering, Why do women stay?

Psychologists seem to agree that there is no clear-cut answer as to why a woman remains in an abusive environment.

But we must realize that why consists of a web of interrelated factors—emotional, legal, religious, psychological, economic, and familial. Herein lies the paradox: Battered wives live a nightmare, yet many never attempt to leave their husbands; often those who do leave return. The more responsible question to ask, then, is not Why does she stay? but What holds her there?"

As a whole, women stay out of feelings of guilt, fear, and a sense of religious duty. They are often victims of learned helplessness which results from feeling helpless, lonely, thinking she can't make it on her own, and feeling that there are no options open to her. Unfortunately, the longer she puts up with the abuse, the more her husband is able to convince her she cannot make it without him, that she has no way out.

Some women stay because they feel responsible for the husband's behavior, certain that they provoked the abuse. Others continue to cling to the hope that he will change. Many Christian wives also feel a sense of spiritual responsibility for their non-Christian husbands.

For many women the motivation to stay is outright fear, knowing that whatever they do they probably cannot escape another explosion. Often such feelings of inadequacy are the result of years of verbal abuse. We can assume that abused women stay with their abusive husbands long after it is no longer safe for them to remain.

According to Fran Porter, director of Sanctuary Home in Waco, Texas, battered women do not believe they can gain escape from the batterer's domination. Unfortunately, they are often right. Even when a woman does consider trying to escape and break out of her fear, she may find that there is no place to go. Until she finds a refuge where she can think clearly, a battered wife will find it difficult to explore her options.

For this reason, I believe the greatest concern for Christian women concerned about the abused woman is to get her to a shelter where she can think clearly and receive the professional guidance and spiritual nourishment needed. Realize, however, that while we can support, comfort, and advise, only the abused wife can determine the ultimate course of action.

Getting Involved

As Christian women embrace the 1990s, we must embrace reality. Domestic violence is a stark reality. We can no longer close our eyes and pretend it isn't there. Ministering to such women "means a willingness not only to stand in the gap by providing for physical services such as child care or temporary housing but also to make a commitment to the long-term process of rebuilding the dignity of a woman whose sense of worth has been utterly shattered."[8]

Perhaps the first thing a woman could do to touch the lives of the battered and bruised is to become familiar with characteristics of the battered woman.

- Has low self-esteem.
- Believes all the myths about battering relationships.
- Is a traditionalist about the home, strongly believes in family unity and the prescribed feminine sex role stereotype.
- Accepts responsibility for the batterer's actions.
- Presents a passive face to the world but has the strength to manipulate her environment enough to prevent further violence and being killed.
- Has severe stress reactions with physical complaints.
- Believes that no one will be able to help her resolve her predicament except herself.[9]

Perhaps you wish to join the multitudes who prefer not to get involved. If so, you may not realize that wife abuse is a felony in all 50 states. However, because the police, the courts, and social agencies traditionally support the privacy of the home, they are often reluctant to interfere in domestic affairs. Yet, can any one of us afford to not link well-thought-out actions to our legitimate concerns? Following are some suggested actions that you can put to work right away.

- Keep in mind that battered women may be murdered by their husbands. Spouse abuse is serious.
- Help the abused to recognize her danger. It is important that she realizes not every woman lives in an abusive situation.
- Become informed. Gather information regarding domestic violence and services in your area that can assist the abused victim.
- Emphasize that the battered woman is not to blame for the abuse, regardless of what precipitated the attack.
- Encourage her to talk. While her story may be unpleasant, it is important that someone listens.
- Focus on her strengths as you help her to realize that she is not helpless.
- Help her realize that God's plan for marriage is not a property arrangement. No husband has ownership rights over his wife.
- Be sensitive not to condemn.
- Let her know that options are available.
- Assure her that it is not God's will that she suffer any form of abuse.
- Help her find a shelter to which she can go. If she decides to leave, help her contact a local emergency shelter or call a hot line.
- Help her plan a strategy. Suggest that if the abuse continues, she needs a plan. Recommend that she put together a suitcase of clothing, important documents (Social Security card, birth certificate, etc.), personal items, and money.
- Pray with her and assure her of your continuous prayer support.
- Emphasize that only she can make a decision regarding the course of action she will take.
- Do not fail to remember that domestic violence is a crime. Failure to intervene can result in the woman's

physical injury or even death. If you suspect a battering incident is occurring, call the police immediately.
- Help her to really believe that with God all things are possible.[10]

Securing a safe emergency shelter is crucial. Shelters are usually the best places for battered women and their children to go. Qualified staff are available to offer support and are trained in counseling victims. For protection of the women, the location of these homes is guarded. You may contact a shelter by calling hot lines, the police department, and community health centers.

Hotels and motels may also serve as temporary shelters. While these are less preferred because they may not be as safe as shelters, women sheltered in hotels and motels do tend not to feel so depressed and isolated. If this is the shelter selected by the abused woman, it is important that someone stays in frequent contact with her in an effort to encourage and support.

In the space below write at least two actions that you can put to work right away.

The following agencies and organizations can provide services and information for the abused or those who wish to minister to an abused woman. Circle at least one agency or service that you will contact this week.

Mental health agency: Offers a variety of types of counseling, including individual and marital.

Social service agencies: Services include child protective services, financial assistance, child care, counseling, payment for emergency shelter, and transportation. Local agencies can make referrals to women's shelters.

Salvation Army: A family services department works with abused women from a Christian perspective.

National Coalition Against Domestic Violence
2401 Virginia Avenue, NW, Suite 306
Washington, DC 20037
(202) 293-8860

Center for the Prevention of Sexual and Domestic Violence
4250 South Mead Street
Seattle, WA 98118
(206) 725-1903

Women Against Violence Emergency Service (WAVES)
(This organization makes referrals to local shelters.)
P. O. Box 1121
Berkeley, CA 94701
(415) 527-HELP

---

[1]Sharlande Sledge, "Profile: Frances Booth Porter," *Folio* 7 (Autumn 1989): 4.

[2]Kay Marshall Strom, *Helping Women in Crisis* (Grand Rapids, MI: Ministry Resources Library, 1986), 145.

[3]Ibid., 143.

[4]James Alsdurf and Phyllis Alsdurf, "Battered into Submission," *Christianity Today* 33 (June 16, 1989): 24.

[5]*Family Violence—The Battered Woman* (Austin, TX: League of Women Voters of Texas Education Fund, 1984).

[6]Ibid.

[7]Alsdurf, "Battered into Submission," 25.

[8]Ibid., 27.

[9]Fran Porter, *Family Violence* conference outline (Birmingham, AL: Woman's Missionary Union), 4.

[10]Strom, *Helping Women in Crisis*, 151-53. Also Porter, *Family Violence* conference outline, 6-7.

8

The Suicide Threat

Though he stumble, he will not fall, for the Lord upholds him with his hand.

Psalm 37:24 (NIV)

I hung up the telephone with feelings of uneasiness and disbelief. For several moments I felt paralyzed. Even my breathing felt shallow. Deep within I knew I couldn't simply sit and wait. I had to do something.

Quickly, I grabbed the telephone receiver as I dialed 911.

"This is the Birmingham emergency unit. How may I help you?"

"My name is Marsha Spradlin. I just received a telephone call from a friend in New York. She is extremely depressed. I have reason to believe that she might try to commit suicide. What do I do? I can't just sit here and wait."

"Calm down. You certainly can't help if you're in a state of panic. First, where in New York does she live?"

"Warsaw."

"Call directory assistance. Ask for the area code for Warsaw, New York. Then call the area code plus 555-1212 for the number of Warsaw's local police department."

"Got it. Thanks."

Within minutes I had made connection with the Warsaw police. Once again, I explained my reason for calling.

"This is Marsha Spradlin. I am calling from Birmingham, Alabama. My friend Andrea Young has just called. I have every reason to believe that she may try to kill herself. She called me about 1 hour ago. She was nearly delirious with depression. She said she didn't want to live any longer. I felt she was reaching out for help.

"Anyway, nothing I said seemed to help. About 30 minutes ago she called again. This time she was obviously intoxicated; I suspect she has taken an overdose of crack. All she said was, 'I want to say good-bye and I love you.' She then hung up. I've tried calling her but I haven't gotten an answer. Can you help?"

"Do you know her address?"

"Yes, can you wait a second? I have a letter from her somewhere on my desk. Here it is. Andrea lives at 1400 Brockbank, apartment 12."

"That's just blocks from the precinct. I'll have a couple of officers check it out right away."

"Please, will you call me as soon as you know something?"

"Of course. Just give the dispatcher your number."

After I hung up, I sat next to the telephone. My mind slipped into reverse, replaying the events of the past four years. She had been doing so well. I sincerely felt that the years of alcohol and drug abuse had finally come to a screeching halt. I suppose the experts are correct. Alcohol and drug abuse is an illness, an illness which never goes away. Instead, this debilitating sickness only goes into remission.

Andrea's brain will never forget that the consumption of certain chemicals can provide a momentary relief or escape from the realities of life. She joins hundreds of thousands who must continue to fight a self-induced propensity toward addiction.

To comfort myself I walked across my office to the bookcase, the one next to my window. I grasped the author's copy of one of my first books, *LIVINGtouch*. I flipped through the pages in search for Andrea's story. As I read I remembered.

I had met Andrea four years earlier while at a women's retreat in Ohio. There was nothing unusual about her. She was cute, young, and looked so very innocent. I suppose two out of three isn't so bad. On second thought, maybe it was bad. She was cute. She was young. But Andrea was far from innocent. As the story of her young life unfolded, I was caught ill prepared. I had never witnessed or ministered to someone whose life was in such shambles.

Andrea was supposed to be in jail during that weekend. However, when she shared with her judge that she had an opportunity to attend a Christian women's retreat, Andrea was released from spending her weekend in jail for drug possession pending she attend the retreat.

I was never quite sure why Andrea and I hit it off. We certainly had little in common. Perhaps the reason was that I had something she needed. But I realized early in our relationship that Andrea wasn't aware that she needed a personal relationship with Jesus Christ.

As we enjoyed our evening meal Andrea shared about her life. I witnessed of Christ's forgiveness and love, but she wasn't ready to trust Him yet. I gave her my address and asked her to write to me. I left her with my confident belief that we would one day be sisters in Christ.

I was right. But that one day did not happen for many months. After dozens of phone calls and volumes of letters, Andrea began to let go of who she was in order to make room for who she could be in Jesus Christ. From a drug rehabilitation center she wrote to me that she was getting better and that she had attended a revival!

"Six weeks later the telephone rang. I had been at the office for only a few minutes. It was Andrea.

" 'Marsha, you won't believe what happened! I just couldn't stand it any longer.'

"Fear entered my mind. 'Oh no, she's back in jail or on drugs.' . . .

" 'Marsha, I called the preacher at 4:00 A.M.. I told him I had to become a Christian. He met me at his office. I accepted Jesus Christ. He told me everything to do. I knew already. . . . But I thought since I had gotten him out of bed, I could at least let him run through it. We're sisters.' "[1]

As I closed my book, I closed my eyes. "Father, let her be OK. Give her hope. Help her to realize that all Christians have problems. But even greater, help her to recognize that all strength and power is hers because of Whose she is."

The sudden ring of the telephone interrupted my prayer.

"Hello. This is Marsha Spradlin."

"Marsha. It's me. Andrea."

"Are you OK? Tell me you are OK."

"It was a close call this time. I don't know what got into me. I'm sorry. I feel that I have let you down. And God. I have let Him down too. The police came. How did they know?"

"Andrea, why did you do it? Why, honey, you have everything to live for."

"Why not, Marsha?" she responded with a weary voice. "I'm lonely up here. I'm tired of being stuck in this house. And nobody really cares anyway."

"Andrea, do you know who called the police?"

"It had to be you."

"That's right. And why, why did I do it?"

"Maybe you were afraid of what I would do?"

"That's right. I had to call. Please understand. I love you. I simply could not *not* do something."

"You mean you cared enough to call the Warsaw police?"

"Of course, I care. But I am not the only one who cares. Jesus Christ still cares, Andrea. You know that, don't you?"

"Yes. I don't know why this happened. But what do I do now?"

"Andrea, don't you think you're very depressed? You know how you get when things aren't going well. You don't see things the way they really are. Honey, I know a lot of people who love you."

"Who? Name them."

"Well, I love you. Don't I count? Then there is Tony."

"Tony and I only fight. I don't know. I know he loves me, but we fight."

"Andrea, I bet all couples have fights when they first get

married. Give it some time. Trust me, Tony loves you.

"Andrea, you tell me. Who else loves you? You know. I have seen you dig deep inside before. God hasn't left you, Andrea. He has been with you all of the time. And He will never leave, no matter how bad things get. I believe He wants to empower you to overcome your depression as well as addiction. Andrea, get your Bible. Find the Scripture verses in Philippians that have helped you before. Will you read them to me?"

As I strained to listen, I could faintly hear Andrea flipping pages. Then I heard her voice.

Not that I have already obtained all this, or have already been made perfect, but I press on to take hold of that for which Christ Jesus took hold of me. Brothers, I do not consider myself yet to have taken hold of it. But one thing I do: Forgetting what is behind and straining toward what is ahead, I press on toward the goal to win the prize for which God has called me heavenward in Christ Jesus" (Phil 3:12-14 NIV).

"Andrea, I vote that we forget what happened today. After all, Christ is willing to forget the moment you ask forgiveness. I'll call you tomorrow, friend. But between now and then let us both pledge to press on!"

Getting INtouch

Life is filled with pain, both physical and psychological, and in so many forms: physical illness, emotional illness, loss, separation, rejection, criticism, accidents, poverty, racism, sexism. The list is endless. Some pain is acute, that is, sudden and short-lived; some pain is chronic in nature, persisting over a long period of time. How we deal with pain is a central issue to the Christian since our Father never said Christians were exempt from pain and suffering.

After coaching my friend through a close call experience,

I realized I needed to know more about suicide. What I learned was painful and sobering.

Suicide has reached epidemic proportions in America. In fact, it is now the eighth leading cause of death. For women, the most vulnerable age for suicide to occur is between 40 and 59.

But women are not the only ones choosing to end their lives. The adolescent suicide rate has tripled during the last generation. In the 1980s one out of every five suicides involved persons between the ages of 15 and 24. Suicide is the second leading cause of death in this age group.

Our children are not immune. "Between the ages of 8 and 14, suicide is the eighth leading cause of death."[2] These are only the documented suicides. Many suicides go unreported or are listed as accidental deaths.

Why do they do it? Actually, suicide seldom stems from just one cause; there are usually many contributing factors. For example, in adolescence the usual feelings of insecurity or alienation are made worse by today's shifting values. Perhaps more than ever people of all ages need a stable support system from their loved ones.

A second reason that many people consider suicide as an option could be our quick-fix society. In a world where everything is automatic and instant, people are convinced that if they have a problem that is not easily solved, the only way out is death.

Third, we lack coping skills. Too many of us, especially when we are depressed, fail to realize that circumstances will change. In Andrea's case, she could not see that her loneliness would not be with her forever.

Fourth, the inescapable fact is that money, security, and personal attractiveness—the things society values—are failing us. Persons who have connected their value, esteem, and worth to tangible commodities are more vulnerable to taking their lives than those who have linked their worth to the eternal fulfillment found in knowing Christ Jesus.

Fifth, those who commit suicide often do not know how to express their feelings or communicate well enough to let other people know how they really feel. They think there is no one to whom they can turn.[3]

Too often family and friends are unaware of the suffering and despair they are feeling until it is too late. This hit home in my life just four years ago. An early morning phone call shook my world as I learned that Jack, my dear friend, had taken his life. I was with him just days before his death. If you had asked me how he was doing, I would have immediately responded, "Great. You know Jack, he's always on top of the world." Unfortunately, Jack is no longer on top of the world. He is dead.

Jack was special to all who loved him. He was the father of two young sons, a loving husband, a deacon in our church, and a community leader. I shall never forget the days that followed his death as each one who loved him experienced the overwhelming guilt that comes when a loved one is lost to suicide.

One remark that clearly stands out was the response of one of Jack's closest friends. "When I get to heaven, I'm going to kick Jack good for what he has done to us." I will never forget wondering why he wanted to kick Jack. Wasn't it obvious that he was living a defeated life, even if we were not aware of his pain?

Kay Marshall Strom points out that suicide is a result of living what we perceive to be an unbearable life. Suicide clearly expresses not so much a desire to die as much as a desperate attempt to get away from the pain of living.

If you and I were to ask a victim who had survived a suicide attempt why she did it, we might be amazed at the answer. "I'm lonesome, depressed."

Let's look closer at the most common cause of suicide, depression. It is estimated that of the people who take their own lives, 60 percent are clinically depressed. For most people depression is not unlike feeling that there is a dark cloud smothering their emotions. For those deeply entangled in the web of depression, life can be debilitating. All too often, in an attempt to be helpful, friends try to jolt the depressed out of their misery. "Come on. Snap out of it."

If you have ever been depressed, you know that you don't just snap out of it. Unfortunately, when the depressed person is unable to reverse her feelings at your request, she often feels even more defeated. Please realize that worthlessness infects both the body and mind. Despondency and lethargy are the results.

Chances are that sometime in your lifetime you will be confronted with the opportunity to share reasons for hope with someone who feels her life is futile.

Getting Involved

Please realize that few suicides just happen. It is possible that they go unrecognized, until it is too late, such as with my friend Jack. However, experts agree that if more people were aware of the symptoms and able to discern the warning signs, fewer deaths would occur. Following is a list of the most common danger signs. Read the list carefully. Read it again and again until these symptoms are permanently inscribed in your mind.
- Preoccupation with death.
- Depression, withdrawal.
- Health problems.
- Change in sleeping and eating patterns.
- Feelings of worthlessness.
- Boredom.
- Difficulty concentrating.
- Lack of interest in future activities.
- Neglect of personal appearance.
- Neglect of upkeep of home.
- Radical personality change.
- Lethargy, fatigue, loss of energy.
- Withdrawal into apathy and helplessness.
- Drug and/or alcohol use.
- Giving away prized possessions and putting affairs in order.

- Cries for help.
- Verbal hints: "I won't be bothering you much longer." "Nothing really matters anymore."
- Asks questions about suicide.
- Becomes suddenly cheerful after a long period of deep depression. This is usually the result of having made the decision to end her life.[4]

If these symptoms describe someone you know, it is imperative that you act and act properly. Below are some do's and don'ts to remember. But this list should not negate seeking professional help from your pastor or qualified health care professional.

DO
- If she has taken an overdose of medication, get her to a medical facility as soon as possible. If possible, find out what medications she has taken and how much.
- Ask questions and be willing to listen.
- Allow her to talk openly without criticism.
- Be supportive and patient.
- Make a distinction between ordinary moodiness and clinical depression.
- Remember, even children get depressed.
- Emphasize that depression is not an indication of mental weakness. Often depression is the result of a physical disorder.
- Assure your Christian friend that depression does not mean God has forsaken her. He still loves and cares for her.
- Assure her that her pain will pass. Depression is not permanent.
- Remind her that no matter how great the hurt, there is always hope.
- Acknowledge that the world is a terrifying place at times, but this does not mean we should give up all hope.
- Assure her that God will never leave or forsake her.

- Point out that, whatever her circumstances, other options are open to her.
- Help her obtain medical help.
- Extend your support.
- Follow up on her progress. Let her know that you really do care.
- Uphold her in your daily prayer.
- Seek professional help of her nearest relative, pastor, or health care professional if the suicidal person is not willing to seek help.[5]

DON'T
- Minimize a suicidal threat or attempt.
- Fault the parents for the depression of children.
- Attempt to change the outlook of a depressed person by admonishing her to cheer up, snap out of it, think about someone worse off. Remember, no one wants to cheer up more than she.
- Say that Christians have no right to be depressed.
- Attempt to council the suicidal person. Instead, direct her to professional help.
- Assure her that her problems will be quickly and permanently overcome. They may be, but they may not be. If not, her disappointment and increased guilt can devastate her even more.[6]

If you know someone whom you feel may be suicidal, it is essential that you not only plan to act—you must act. Reread the list of symptoms on pages 99-100. In the following space write all symptoms that clearly describe the person(s) you suspect is suicidal. In addition, write any additional symptom or bizarre behavior that has heightened your concern. This information will be helpful when seeking professional support.

Reread the do's and don'ts listed on pages 100-101. Plan your strategy. In the following space write actions that you can implement right away.

Actions I will take:

1.

2.

3.

4.

5.

Check local listings of psychological health care services in your telephone book. Write the name of the service and telephone number here.

For more information on mental illness and suicide, contact

National Institute of Mental Health
5600 Fisher Lane
Parklawn Building, Room 15C17
Rockville, MD 20857
(301) 443-4513

[1]Marsha Spradlin, *LIVINGtouch* (Birmingham: New Hope, 1988), 31.
[2]Kay Marshall Strom, *Helping Women in Crisis* (Grand Rapids, MI: Ministry Resources Library, 1986), 114.
[3]Ibid., 115.
[4]Ibid., 118-19.
[5]Ibid., 120-21.
[6]Ibid., 121-22.

9

Counting the Cost

"For I was hungry and you gave me something to eat, . . . I was a stranger and you invited me in." . . . "I tell you the truth, whatever you did for one of the least of these brothers of mine, you did for me."

Matthew 25:35,40 (NIV)

Michelle lives with her mother and four children in a small windowless one-room apartment in south Dallas. The run-down apartment contains two inexpensive aluminum pots, four worn blankets that serve as a makeshift mattress, and a kerosene stove for cooking. An assortment of cardboard boxes are used as storage space for a few cans of groceries and clothing. Michelle has been without steady employment for over two years. To supplement her food stamps, Michelle and her mother collect aluminum cans and other discarded items.

But to many Michelle is one of the luckier ones. At least she has shelter. As many as 3 million people go to bed every night on sidewalks that meander throughout overpopulated cities. But having a place to call home isn't the only reason Michelle is lucky. She has obtained one of life's most important possessions—*hope!*

Hope for Michelle comes twice a week as she, her mother, and four small children join over 200 other helpless individuals whose empty eyes brighten as they stand in line to receive hot soup and a smile. This feeding station is located underneath a freeway bridge just six blocks from her home. Pat, a professional woman who lives and works in downtown

Dallas, volunteers her time, energy, and emotions to deliver hope to the hopeless.

"I've seen the hopelessness, helplessness, gratitude, belligerence, and empty eyes which speak of empty hearts. I've cried over the children's emaciated bodies which remind me of the starving children in Ethiopia. And I've rejoiced when I learn that just one of our regulars has found a job.

"Pouring hot soup into a bowl may seem like a small thing to many Christians, but it is my way of communicating the good news of Jesus Christ to people like Michelle, people who have potential, but who are so burdened by the realities of life that their only spark of hope seems to have smoldered out. The key, I think, is to package God's love in gifts that meet basic human needs. For the people under this bridge, hope is delivered in a plastic throwaway bowl. Gifts of hope don't have to come in the form of food. Hopes comes in so many shapes and sizes. As a Christian, my responsibility is to use what gifts, resources, and abilities God has given me to touch the lives of those who are often labeled untouchable.

"But before I can touch their lives in Jesus' name, I must first remove my spiritual blinders. I must be brave enough to see the world as it is. I must probe beyond the obvious. When I do I see the needs everywhere, in every city, in everybody's world. I cannot escape knowing about needs as newscast after newscast features the all-too-often plight of the growing number of homeless and helpless.

"For years I insisted on hiding behind my spiritual blinders, refusing to see the insidious needs lurking in virtually every corner of my world. Why doesn't the government do something? I wondered. Little did I know that government officials were asking, Why doesn't the church do something?

"While it takes little effort to realize needs, it takes extraordinary courage to reach out in Jesus' name. As I respond to needs by delivering tiny bowls of hope to people like Michelle, I am cutting across cultural, social, and emotional barriers. And, while I am certainly not in this for what it can do for me, I must underscore that I have never been as happy or more fulfilled than when I pour morsels of hope into Michelle's empty cup."

Unfortunately, Michelle is not alone in her quest for the necessities of life: food and shelter. Michelle is joined by millions of other women who are victims of life itself. Another victim is Susan McPheason.

Susan never dreamed she would face this. In a matter of months the life she had known began to crumble. Now she calls a church shelter home.

"When I first came here it frightened me. I didn't think I was like these people. I had always had a home to live in. When I became like the rest of these people, it really humbled me. I began to realize that I was just another person who was no better than anyone else. Until I became homeless, my idea of the homeless was the typical stereotype. You know, someone on drugs or an alcoholic. I didn't realize that the homeless included people just like me, people with families and small children. Please, don't put down people who do not have a place to live. We need your help. We are sad and depressed. If only someone would just listen."

Fortunately for Susan, someone did listen. Marsha Tanner is a volunteer working in a shelter provided by the Memorial Drive Baptist Center, Atlanta, Georgia. By working with the homeless Marsha has discovered their greatest need.

"The people who come to the shelter do need someone who will sincerely listen. They have so many problems and such a long way to go. While I know that Christ is the answer, I also know that what these dear people need is someone to show them of Christ's love. Showing sometimes takes a long time because while they are hungry and homeless they can't hear."

Marsha has learned firsthand the frustrations of working at a shelter. There is so much work to be done and so few volunteers.

"I feel the biggest excuse for not volunteering is 'I don't have time.' I have five children and I know how much time there is not in a day. But the Lord has given us a perfect example—the loaves and the fishes. 'If you will give a little bit to me, I can do a lot.' Just watching the Father do this has been my biggest blessing. I am doing what the Lord has told me to do at this time in my life. You see, I know that any one of these people could be me. There is no guarantee that you or I won't one day be among one of the homeless people in the world."

Fortunately, Marsha is not the only woman in the Atlanta area who has recognized the needs of the homeless, helpless, and hungry. Nearly halfway across Atlanta's Peachtree area lives Elizabeth Beane. Elizabeth is very aware of the identity of the homeless.

During a business trip to Atlanta last fall, I made arrangements to visit with Elizabeth. In a taped interview Elizabeth shared how she became involved with homeless women in her area.

"Our church is an older established church in Atlanta. In the early 1970s our church community found itself in a transition. We began to see more and more homeless people coming by looking for a place to stay. In 1984 we rented our gymnasium to the Christian council for $1.00 per year. The gym was to become a shelter for homeless women in our area.

"The day the shelter opened 99 women and children sought refuge. Imagine row after row of beds and personal belongings inside a gymnasium with basketball goals and bleachers. It took only one night to realize that this was not what we needed. No one could sleep in such a situation. Each day the needs increased. Neither the facility nor the space was adequate.

"While the women and children who came to the facility were from a variety of backgrounds, all of the women who found themselves homeless had one thing in common. None of them woke up one morning and simply decided they wanted to be homeless. Their condition is really the result of many factors. Of course drugs and alcohol are factors, but a not-so-obvious factor is illness.

"In the fall of 1986 our church joined forces with the

Christian Council of Metropolitan Atlanta to support a dream—a dream that would provide more than just a bandage for homeless women. The dream came to be known as the Anchor Center. An anchor means hope. And our center brings hope to countless women. The center offers a holistic residential and transitional program designed to help homeless women move from their present tenuous state to a more permanent environment by returning them to the mainstream of society as productive, contributing individuals; provide reinforcement to help them secure employment, affordable living accommodations, and become self-sustaining through career training and skill development programs; and create an environment of hope and renewed vigor for life.

"Before we were in a position to put hope into action there was much work to be done. Much of the structure had been built in the late 1950s. The entire third floor was falling into disrepair because of lack of use. We took the small Sunday School rooms and renovated them into living quarters. And what used to be assembly areas are now living rooms for all of the families. The preschooler's department is now the laundry room. Other Sunday School classrooms were transformed into bedrooms. After bathing facilities were added in February 1988, the Anchor Center opened its doors.

"Our work has flourished. Instead of simply housing homeless women, we serve in a supportive role as we help these women find jobs and seek spiritual guidance. We help our women find a church home after they leave Anchor. Because of the program support, at least 85 percent of the women who go through Anchor get back on their feet. And since the day the shelter opened in February 1988, 98 women and 225 children have resided at Anchor. While seeing such a large number of women respond positively to our program is affirming, becoming involved in the program is not always a positive experience. If you feel God is leading you to become involved with the homeless, the hungry, and the down-and-out, you have to risk being involved; and risk meaning risking being hurt."

"Elizabeth, you said drugs and alcohol are factors which impact homelessness. Is there any other factor?"

"Pain. The homeless so often are hurting themselves, and their hurt is often a result of being hurt. Very often they have been physically abused by a husband or boyfriend. And, almost always, they are emotionally abused. They feel they are worthless.

"Abuse is a tricky thing. While they may be physically or emotionally abused by their husbands, I mean physically beaten, at least 35 percent leave our shelter only to go back into a situation where they are abused. Why? At least at home they have food and shelter. And they are so beaten down, literally, and emotionally scarred that they do not think they can make it on their own. They have been told they are worthless for so long that they believe it. Many simply do not feel they deserve anything better.

"Often they know nothing of God's love. Many have never experienced a family in the true sense of the word. Often I have reached out to minister only to have the one I am so wanting to help turn her back on me. 'What's in this for you?' she asks.

"What's in it for me? Plenty. You see, when even one woman makes it, learns to stand on her own two feet, develops a network of friends that can support her, and connects with a caring church, well, it is worth it all."

Getting INtouch

Two of the greatest problems in America today are homelessness and poverty. It is estimated that as many as 3 million people wander the streets of our cities with nowhere to sleep and nothing to eat.

Who are the homeless? A general definition of homelessness must include anyone whose primary nighttime residence is a public or private shelter, an emergency lodging housing, a commercial hotel or motel, or any other public space.

Being homeless means more than not having shelter, however. Being homeless means not having a place to save the things that connect the homeless to their past. It means losing all contact with friends and family, uprooting children from school, having your pet put in a pound. Being homeless means accepting handouts from strangers and depending upon government agencies for survival.[1]

The old stereotype of the single, white male alcoholic, the so-called Skid Row derelict, no longer applies. The face of America's homeless now mirrors the faces of America's poor women and their children.

Recently the Institute of Medicine issued a report which claims that "the homeless population now includes higher proportions of women and minority members, such as blacks and Hispanics, and a growing number of people with full-time jobs." The fastest growing group among the many subpopulations of the homeless include children under the age of 18, usually as part of a family headed by a mother.[2]

Government officials are concerned and are studying this problem. Many social agencies are asking, Where are the churches? All too often churches do not see this problem. Could it be that churches simply are unaware of the homeless people in their own neighborhood, or are our churches playing the game of hide-and-seek?

Where are the homeless? As expected, large numbers of homeless persons are in our major large cities, but not restricted to them. Homeless persons are anywhere and everywhere—public parks, transportation terminals, cars. "Less noticeable are the hidden homeless—the people who have not yet had to take refuge on the streets, but live doubled or tripled up with relatives or friends in some temporary, makeshift arrangement."[3]

How much do you know about homelessness? Test your knowledge by reading the following statements. Write a *T* next to each statement that you feel is true. Write an *F* in the space next to statements you believe to be false.

TRUE OR FALSE

___ About 40 percent of the homeless are families with children.

___ About 14 percent of the homeless are single women.

___ There are more than 500,000 homeless children in the United States.

___ The average age of a homeless child is six years old.

___ The number of homeless in America will rise 25 percent this year.

___ The homeless are more subject to certain diseases and have more trouble getting health care than other citizens.

___ Homeless children suffer more from chronic physical disorders and illnesses than children in the general population.

___ Homeless children seem to suffer greater emotional and developmental problems.

___ The two most common health problems among individual homeless adults are alcohol-related problems and mental disorders.

___ Drug abuse appears to be increasing. Approximately 25 to 40 percent of homeless men have serious alcohol problems; about one-third of individual homeless adults have a major mental disorder.

___ Illness can cause hunger and homelessness; for example, a person with AIDS becomes too sick to work and loses the means to pay for housing.

___ Illness is often the result of homelessness. People living on the street or in a shelter are at high risk for a variety of health problems such as poor circulation, skin diseases, tuberculosis, and dental disease.[4]

___ The homeless and hungry are at high risk for traumatic injuries because they are frequently victims of violent crimes such as rape, assault, and attempted robbery.[5]

___ Homeless people also have a harder time following a doctor's orders when they do receive attention. People who have to carry all their worldly goods with them on the streets by day, eat in soup kitchens, and perhaps sleep in a different place every night find it difficult or

110

impossible to get bed rest, follow a special diet, or keep to a schedule for taking medication.[6]

__ One of 7 Americans lives in poverty. This represents 13.5 percent of the population, or 32.5 million Americans. Another 11 million live within 25 percent of the poverty level.

__ Forty-four million Americans struggle to provide the essentials of life—food, shelter, utilities, medical and dental care, clothing, and transportation.

__ Two-thirds of all the poor are white. The poverty rates by race are 10.5 percent whites, 33 percent blacks, 28 percent Hispanics, and 18 percent other races.

__ The South has twice the poverty level of the North.

__ The United States is the only industrialized nation in the world in which children comprise the largest segment of the poverty population.

If you answered true to all questions, you were right. The statements listed above paint a grim picture of life for millions of Americans. And while such a picture is dismal to even the most optimistic, it is imperative that we never give up hope. Could it be that someone's well-being and welfare depends on how you choose to package hope?

Getting Involved

Before getting involved with the hungry and homeless, we must rediscover what Jesus said. Turn in your Bible to Matthew 5:3. In the following space write the words spoken by Jesus.

Stop for a moment and think about these questions: Could it possibly be that we are the poor in spirit? Is it possible that our souls are in need of spiritual nourishment? I believe that as we get involved with those in need, our own souls are nourished. If you want to work alongside Jesus, you may want to consider meeting Him in the soup kitchen.

Get involved by discovering the needs in your community. Many agencies can give you suggestions of how you can become involved with ministering to the homeless and poor. Such trusted agencies include your local school system, as well as social and government agencies who serve the poor.

Second, link up with other churches and government and community agencies that provide assistance and ministries to the poor.

Third, increase your voluntary giving to various hunger funds provided by your church.

Fourth, denounce existing prejudices, bigotry, and bias against the poor and homeless. Such a position is contagious.

Fifth, create other ministry alternatives rather than only emergency assistance. Examples include literacy education and conversational English, tutoring programs through your public schools, credit unions for the poor, health care services, child-care services for working mothers and for those in educational or skill improvement courses, job training and placement services, adequate housing, and advocacy.

Sixth, work on your theology. Study God's Word regarding the poor. Our theology should not promise success and prosperity, but it should lead us to minister and to serve in Jesus' name.

Seventh, write your congressman and community leaders suggesting that state and community funds be made available to operate facilities where homeless people can safely convalesce from nonemergency illness.

Eighth, never forget "whatever you did for one of the least of these brothers of mine, you did it for me."

In the following space write all actions you are ready to take.

For more information on homelessness in America and ways to become involved, write to:

National Coalition for the Homeless
105 East 22nd Street
New York, NY 10010
(212) 460-8110

or

1419 Rhode Island Avenue, NW
Washington, DC 20005
(202) 659-3310

Clearing House on Homelessness Among Mentally Ill People (CHAMP)
8630 Fenton Street, Suite 300
Silver Springs, MD 20910
(301) 588-5484

National Volunteer Hotline
1 (800) HELP-664
Operated by the Community for Creative Non-Violence (CCNV)
452 2nd Street, NW
Washington, DC 20001

---

[1]"Homelessness in America: A Summary" (Washington, DC: National Coalition for the Homeless): 1.
[2]"The Unhealthy Homeless," *The Futurist* (July-August 1989): 56.
[3]"Homelessness in America: A Summary," 1.
[4]"The Unhealthy Homeless," 56.
[5]Ibid., 56-57.
[6]Ibid., 57.

10

Courage to Care

"I was in prison and you came to visit me." . . . *"I tell you the truth, whatever you did for one of these brothers of mine, you did for me."*

Matthew 25:36,40 (NIV)

Pat sat in her car ten minutes before she found enough courage to follow through with her commitment. Nervously, she opened the car door. The icy wind seemed to suck out her already shallow breath. With due precaution, Pat walked toward the guard's station at the correctional center gate. With a watchful eye glaring into the morning sun she noticed the tall man approaching her. Fear intensified as he walked toward her. She stopped and strained to see who he was. "Ah, it is only the guard." Relief created a surge of confidence and courage—treasured emotions.

As the guard walked toward her, Pat reached inside her purse for the letter and handed the envelope to him. After careful inspection, the guard dropped the envelope on the small desk located inside the guard station. From a tiny window shielded by bars, Pat watched his every move. She silently shivered as he picked up a telephone receiver to inform the correctional center authorities of her arrival.

Finally, the guard unlocked the first set of double barbed wire gates that separated freedom from captivity. Pat walked inside. I think I'll let her tell the story now.

"Those first steps were the hardest. I had never been inside a correctional center before. The steel and concrete were a dull, gray reminder of not only where I was but where I was not. After the guards inspected my purse, I was escorted to a small room. The room was completely empty except for a small table, two chairs, and a large clock hanging on the gray wall. The emptiness caused even my breath to echo.

"I stared at the clock. The wait seemed like an eternity. Yet the moment the door opened I jumped to my feet as if I were not expecting a visitor. But as the door slowly opened, I felt His presence rush inside the cold, tiny room where I sat alone.

"Juanita wasn't anything like I had expected. Other than her correctional center uniform, I would say she did not look much different from me. As soon as I looked into her eyes, I knew I was not alone in my fear. Immediately I sensed that Juanita was perhaps as afraid of me as I was of her. But as the moment turned into minutes, both of us began to drop our guard. Moment by moment Juanita and I began to let go and let each other inside our hearts. As we exchanged our thoughts, our fears dissipated. And in the cold void where fear once resided was the possession of a new friend, a friend who cared as much about me as I cared for her."

"But why, Pat? Why did you do it? I am terrified by the idea of initiating a relationship with an inmate."

"I used to feel the same way, Marsha. Realize that my decision to sponsor an inmate wasn't one I made overnight. Let me back up.

"You might say I had come to the conclusion that words without deeds are empty. I am what some call a paid Christian, that is, I am in full-time Christian service. I began to realize that I could not continue to teach and encourage others to be involved in mission action unless I was willing to be involved myself.

"My first contact with the women at the correctional center in Raleigh was at Christmas. My office learned that many of the women in the correctional center did not receive even one gift, much less a visit during the Christmas holidays. For that reason several women in my office decided to investigate the possibility of sponsoring women inmates in the correctional center located in our city. Our ideas and enthusiasm grew. What started as one or two women in our office sponsoring one or two women grew, giving every woman in our state organization an opportunity to participate in the Christmas sponsorship program. Our first step was meeting with correctional center officials. The officials were nearly as excited about the possibilities as were we. By the end of our first meeting, the officials had given us a list of items that would be allowed within the correctional center's compound.

"The Christmas sponsorship program was an unprecedented success. Instead of having an office Christmas party, we spent that time stuffing stockings with goods received from women living between North Carolina's eastern Atlantic coast and western Great Smoky Mountains.

"During the months that followed, many staff members in our office, as well as women living throughout our state, stayed in touch with the inmates that we had met at the Christmas party sponsored by our state. Likewise, our office staff stayed in touch with the correctional center officials regarding needs. The officials soon realized that we were serious about ministering to these forgotten women. It was at this point that the correctional center authorities issued a challenge unlike any before.

"We were asked to sponsor inmates. Sponsorship would include visiting the inmate at the correctional center as well as taking the inmate out two or three times a week. Of course, the inmates who qualified had earned the privilege. The sponsorship program was not something we took lightly.

"After prayerful consideration, I agreed to apply. Making application meant filling out multitudes of forms, giving addresses of every place I had ever lived during the past 15 years, as well as listing dozens of character references. Completing the paperwork was the first hurdle, which was followed by a legal screening investigation.

"After several weeks, I received notice that I had been cleared to be a sponsor of an inmate. To be honest, my feelings were split. I was thrilled, yet terrified.

"While every visit with Juanita was special, I shall always cherish the first hour we spent together. We talked just as any two people who wanted to get to know one another. I shared about my family and Juanita shared about hers. I was astonished to learn that Juanita and I were more alike than different. We both grew up in a rural area of North Carolina. Our fathers both worked in the mill. Our home lives were nearly identical.

"I shall never forget her reply when I asked what she wanted to do during our first opportunity to leave the correctional center compound.

" 'I want to wash dishes.'

" 'Wash dishes? You have been here eight years and all you want to do is to wash dishes?'

" 'Yes. You see, each morning I look outside my window through the barbed wire fence and try to remember what it is like to be on the other side. The most natural thing I can remember is standing at my kitchen sink washing dishes. I bet I've imagined washing a million dishes during these eight years.'

"With each visit I realized just how much Juanita and I did have in common, except wanting to wash dishes. As hard as it was to do, I had to force myself to remember that which we did not have in common. Juanita had a criminal status. Like the majority of women at the correctional center, Juanita found herself in situations and circumstances profoundly different than anything I had ever experienced.

"Before Juanita came into my life, I found it easy to judge others. But after hearing Juanita's story, I realized that I would be hard pressed to say what I would do in her particular situation. Because I do not know what I would have done if I truly walked in her shoes, I did become convinced that I was not in a position to be her judge.

"Nothing describes Juanita's tragedy better than simply

being at the wrong place at the wrong time. Juanita's husband, Frank, robbed a convenience store. She was in their truck when the crime was committed. As a result, she was the accessory to the crime, resulting in having to serve the same number of years as her husband.

"Situations like these cause a lot of tension in the correctional center. Women who were accessories to a crime and women who actually committed a crime both share the same correctional center experience. This, many feel, is an inequality in the justice system.

"Two weeks after our initial get-acquainted visit at the correctional center, I made arrangements to take Juanita out on a two-hour pass. The morning before our outing, I called Juanita's social worker to make the necessary arrangements. I asked the social worker to give Juanita a note:

Juanita:
Be thinking about what you want for supper. We'll stop by the grocery store on the way home. I'll cook. You wash the dishes!
> Your friend,
> Pat

"It took over an hour to complete the paperwork necessary for Juanita's two-hour pass. By the time we were outside the gate, we were both ravenous. Juanita said little. But her eyes revealed deep emotions.

"I stopped by the grocery store just blocks from my house to buy the necessary ingredients for our meal. Juanita reached deep into her pocket for a small slip of paper listing everything needed for her favorite meal, country fried steak and gravy. The meal was wonderful and the fellowship not unlike two friends who had known and trusted each other for a lifetime. While the moments clipped by, we were careful not to be one second late returning to the center. We both knew that our prompt respect of curfew would grant us another visit.

"As I drove home after returning Juanita to the correc-

118

tional center, my thoughts and feelings seemed locked in midemotion. It had not occurred to me the numerous living experiences that Juanita had missed. On that eventful Saturday I introduced my new friend to an automatic bank teller machine, an oven which heats in seconds, and a drive-through car wash.

" 'They won't believe this,' I remember her saying.

" 'Believe what?'

" 'I know this sounds crazy, but I can't wait to get back to the correctional center to tell my friends about all that's happened since we've been in. Life's gone on without us.'

"Juanita was right. Life had gone on. While I could not speak for the other 500 inmates at the correctional center, I could speak for Juanita. But as far as I was concerned, life would never go on without her again.

"The months and years that followed delivered many such visits. With each visit our friendship grew. I shall never forget Juanita sharing her feelings after a shopping spree one Saturday morning. As she wiped a single tear, Juanita shared:

" 'You must know how wonderful it is to walk around a store like a real person.'

"Holidays and birthdays all were special events. I soon found myself taking Juanita to church. It was then I realized that Juanita was a Christian. Freely we shared our experiences with Jesus Christ.

" 'I would have never made it during these eight years had it not been for God. Don't get me wrong, I'm no saint, but I do know God loves me. He shows me every day, especially in you.' "

Getting INtouch

"This thing of giving I do not understand, any more than you do. There is something about it that blesses us. . . . Those who give most have most left. . . . I believe that everyone who dried a tear will be spared the shedding of a thousand tears. . . . I believe that every sacrifice we make will so enrich us in the future that our regret will be that we did not sacrifice the more. . . . Give—and somewhere, from out of the clouds, or from the sacred depths of human hearts, a melody divine will reach your ears, and gladden all your days upon this earth."[1]

George F. Burba, whose words you have just read, is not a theologian. But it is obvious to me that he has an astute and unyielding opinion regarding the value of giving yourself to others in Christ's name. Like Pat, he has come to recognize that virtually every aspect of the human experience has been enormously affected by those who give their time, their love, and their life unselfishly to others.

Health care agencies, colleges, welfare, research institutions, and churches are but a few places where Americans interact every day with the volunteer sector. Could it be that the multicolored threads of doing unto others have become so tightly woven with who we are as a people that we are no longer aware of the extraordinary strength and diversity that giving to others plays in the human experience?

Philanthropy, giving to others, is certainly not a modern invention. Concern for one another goes back to ancient times. But even then incentives for altruistic deeds were as distinctive as each one's life. Deeds through which philanthropic motivations were expressed have changed greatly in modern times. Such changes reflect alterations in thinking, social structures, and the practicality of available opportunities.

A quick review of early volunteerism reveals that nothing affected the ancient volunteer movement as did communication and transportation. In fact, centuries ago concern regarding hunger and illness for those "across the water" was never heard. As communication and transportation ushered in the technological age, volunteers were on hand, ready, willing, and able to receive the message and respond to it.

While it is worth noting that the volunteer movement played a significant role in ushering in the Reformation as

120

well as the origin of a new country, all evidence indicates that the relationship between the volunteer and the church was the foundation on which the Church of our Lord, Jesus Christ, was built. In fact, through the years no group has changed society through their volunteer efforts as has Christ's Church.

Why such coexistence between the church and volunteerism? The answer is clearly tucked in the pages of the New Testament. If we could escape the moment and let our eyes compare the Old Testament to the New Testament, we could clearly identify the various benefits of volunteer laity in the church and community.

"In the Old Testament the priestly duties were limited to the tribes of Levi. In the New Testament the priestly functions were the responsibility of the entire church."[2]

In other words, Christ has declared that all believers constitute this royal priesthood. From the earliest tradition of the Old Testament, some of the priests have been ordained, or called out, to perform certain special functions, but 99 percent of the priesthood is unordained laity. Ministry is the work of the whole priesthood; and it involves being called by the Holy Spirit to do six things: proclaim, teach, worship, love, witness, and serve.

The New Testament makes it clear that every Christian is to apply his or her gifts in the pursuit of the Christian mission. First Peter 2:9 underscores this position, making it clear that the work of the church is not to be left up to a chosen few, but to all of God's people.

The particular nature of each Christian's responsibility is succinctly described in Ephesians 4:16 (TLB). This Scripture verse emphasizes the mandate that the life and work of the church is the responsibility of all.

Under his direction the whole body is fitted together perfectly, and each part in its own special way helps the other part, so that the whole body is healthy and growing and full of love.

While the use of volunteers in the church has become the Church's greatest strength, the lack of volunteers has been described by some as the Church's weakest link.

Why such an emphasis on the use of laity? Not only is the use of volunteer leadership a biblical mandate but also a practical necessity.

Why does a person volunteer? Seldom does a person volunteer for one particular reason. More often a combination of motivations sparks one toward volunteering. Adequate motivation for voluntary service falls somewhere between need and opportunity, which should make an adequate appeal to every Christian. This motivation may be supplemented by fellowship of the workers, attractive working conditions, or even a dignified and personal invitation. Normally, a person accepts a volunteer responsibility because of a triggered event. The event may be a friend's request, a contact by a committee member, or a response to public appeal. In Pat's case, her volunteer response came as a result of two factors: a divine mandate and personal observation of a need.

Americans have always been distinguished as a nation wanting to give. In a recent survey, "donations by individuals to charitable institutions are the highest they have been in 17 years."[3] Why such an upward trend? A report launched by the National Center for Citizen Involvement suggests that the 1970s may have introduced a new era in volunteerism, that Americans are tired of being self-absorbed, and in record numbers are finding creative ways to reach out to others.

Another reason for the shift toward philanthropy is the interaction between two threads, the shift toward more traditional values, and the increase in leisure time.

Who will be the volunteers in the future? It could be you, my friend. Future decades project that volunteerism will become a family activity as families sacrifice vacation activities to participate in volunteer projects. Education has been a key factor in the increase of volunteerism in the past decades. Since a full 65 percent of college graduates now volunteer, and since the projected educational level in decades to come is high, so will be the degree of volunteerism.

In summary, senior adults, women, and Protestants remain leaders in the volunteer movement of this era. And while volunteerism may be at an all-time high, predictions are strong that the movement may continue its upward swing. The volunteer pendulum may swing in favor of family involvement as well as the involvement of the educated. Yet it is my opinion that we must not let go of our momentum—women! As we trace the life history of women living along the Mediterranean Sea during Jesus' day, we realize that women have always led the way in ministering and witnessing to others in Christ's name. I believe women will always pave the way for altruistic contribution to the world in the name of our Lord.

Getting Involved

Needs are plentiful. One does not have to look very hard or go very far to identify someone in need. Likewise, nothing lessens our load as does ministering to one whose burden makes our own burdens feel light. Too often, however, we become too involved in our own lives, the blessed as well as bleak, to recognize the needs of those living near us. I am firmly convinced that in order to make room for a needy person, I must first stop demanding that my own needs be met.

"OK," you say. "Where do I sign up?"

While certain volunteer effort may involve signing up, ministering to those in need does not require a contract. Instead, volunteering your time and energy to embrace those in need requires only a true commitment. Like Pat, commitment usually comes when we realize that God's mandate was written with me in mind.

"But I'm not trained," you say. "I don't have the necessary skills." Most often, skills in caring are learned by doing. Again, Pat's ministry to Juanita is an example.

"You don't understand my case. I simply do not know anyone in need," you say. While I personally feel this excuse is only an excuse, perhaps there are 2 or 3 individuals out of our world of 5 billion people who do not know someone in need. If you are one of these rare individuals, allow me to submit just a few suggestions.

1. Call your minister. His vocation in life puts him in touch with needy individuals every day. Perhaps he has a suggestion of someone in your community who would benefit from your benevolence.

2. If your community has a nursing home, chances are good that you could volunteer a couple of hours a day or a week visiting an elderly person who is without family or human concern.

3. Call your local Department of Human Resources (listings may vary; check your telephone yellow or blue pages). If you have a couple of free hours a week and a skill, your services are needed. Opportunities for service include helping elderly individuals fill out income tax documents, providing transportation for homebound, participating in community-sponsored programs such as Meals on Wheels, telephone hot line answering services, etc.

4. Call your local denomination's association, council, or fellowship of churches regarding programs needing your support. Programs may include teaching English as a second language to international students and/or refugees as well as a variety of mission action projects.

5. Look in the yellow pages of your phone book for listing of helping agencies that need volunteers to suggest and conduct their work.

6. Hospitals are another excellent place to donate volunteer services. The Department of Human Resources is a good place to start.

7. Don't forget your church. Remember, the church is only as strong as its laity.

The list of possibilities seems endless. While not all suggestions listed here are directly related to a local church, and some do not allow proselytizing by volunteers, all volunteer programs do put you in a position to nurture a relationship with a needy person on behalf of Jesus Christ. As you invest your time in the lives of others, you are fulfilling Christ's mandate! Remember, "Whatever you did for one of these brothers of mine, you did for me" (Matt. 25:40 NIV).

In the following space write all actions you are ready to take. Next to the action write when you plan to carry out this action.

For more information

National Volunteer Hotline
1 (800) HELP-664
Operated by the Community for Creative Non-Violence (CCNV)
452 2nd Street, NW
Washington, DC 20001

---

[1]Arnaud C. Marts, *Philanthrophy's Role in Civilization* (New York: Harper and Row, Publishers, Inc., 1953), chap. 2, quoted in Brian O'Connell, ed., *America's Voluntary Spirit* (New York: The Foundation Center, 1983), 143.
[2]Reginald M. McDonough, *Working with Volunteer Leaders in the Church* (Nashville: Broadman Press, 1976), 10.
[3]"Research Alert" 6 (January 6, 1989):2.

Epilogue

Calling All Women to Proclaim

Then Jesus answered and said to her, O woman, your faith is great.

Matthew 15:28 (NASB)

December 31, 1989

This is the moment I have dreamed would come. The first draft of *INtouch* (Women of Faith in the 90s) is finished! I feel the exhilarating charge of energy and excitement which comes when a hefty task is completed. It is a timely completion, I feel. As I glance at my watch, I realize that we are within moments of the dawning of the decade called the nineties. In fact, in less than 32 minutes 1989 will be history.

Yet, sandwiched in between the thrills of having written are unresolved feelings. I feel the task has only begun. During these months of researching, listening, and writing, I have not only come INtouch with the lives of others, I have come INtouch with myself in a new, unsettling way. No longer is it good enough to simply enjoy having written a book that will be read by women like you. Instead, I find myself needing to step to the side in order to ask some rather sobering questions.

"Lord, who among us is the greatest? Is it Jessie or Georgia, Teresa or Pat? Which one of these women of faith really knows the depths of Your heart?"

Just as He spoke to the Twelve on the eve of His Cru-

126

cifixion, I can hear Him sweetly speak on this eve, "but let him who is the greatest among you become as the youngest, and the leader as the servant."

As this present moment is captured by tomorrow, I hear our Father calling each of us, women of faith, to proclaim hope. Perhaps you are wondering, But how do I fit into His plan to spread hope to the lost, the hurting, the hungry, the hopeless? As never before, I am convinced that He has chosen to use each of us, not just the young whose influence seems keen, not just the middle-aged woman whose stability is intact, and not just the older woman whose wisdom has ripened with time. He has chosen all of us!

Before you close this book, you have some choices to make. What are you going to do now? Are you simply planning to place your book on a shelf, feeling proud that you have read a book from cover to cover? Or will you pass it on to a friend? Better still, will you acknowledge that our Father needs you to touch the lives of ordinary women you know who are living ordinary lives?

As women of faith may we embrace this moment. May we recognize that God has gifted us with this day to use as we will. The choice of how we will invest this day is ours to make. When tomorrow has come and gone, may it be said of us, "We were faithful to our call."

As you go to reach out to others in His name, be assured of my prayers.

Resources

Chapter 1
Crossing Generations

Allen, Catherine B. *A Century to Celebrate*. Birmingham, AL: Woman's Missionary Union, 1987.

McLaughlin, Steven D., Barbara D. Melber, John O. G. Billy, Denise M. Zimmerle, Linda D. Winges, Terry R. Johnson. *The Changing Lives of American Women*. Chapel Hill, NC: University of North Carolina Press, 1988.

Ryan, Mary P. *Womanhood in America: From Colonial Times to the Present*. New York: Franklin Watts, Inc., 1983.

Chapter 2
Countdown into the Twenty-first Century

Ashker, Helene. *Jesus Cares for Women*. Colorado Springs, CO: NavPress, 1987.

Bellah, Mike. *Baby Boom Believers*. Wheaton, IL: Tyndale House Publishers, 1988.

Finzel, Hans. *Help! I'm a Baby Boomer*. Wheaton, IL: Victor Books, 1989.

Naisbitt, John. *Megatrends*. New York: Warner Books, 1982.

Russell, Cheryl. *100 Predictions for the Baby Boom: The Next 50 Years*. New York: Plenum Press, 1987.

Chapter 3
Closing the Image Gap

Cunningham, Richard B. *Creative Stewardship*. Nashville: Abingdon, 1979.

Eller, Vernard. *The Simple Life*. Grand Rapids, MI: Wm. B. Eerdmans Publishing Company, 1973.

Fagan, A. R. *What the Bible Says About Stewardship*. Nashville: Convention Press, 1976.

Hendricks, William L., ed. *Resource Unlimited*. Nashville: Stewardship Commission of the Southern Baptist Convention, 1972.

Rogers, Mary, and Nancy Joyce. *Women and Money*. New York: McGraw-Hill Book Company, 1978.

Wachtel, Paul L. *The Poverty of Affluence*. New York: Free Press, 1983.

Chapter 4
Facing Addiction

Dobson, James. *Love Must Be Tough*. Waco, TX: Word Books, 1983.

Drews, Toby R. *Getting Them Sober*. South Plainfield, NJ: Bridge Publishing, Inc., 1980.

Minirth, Frank, and Paul D. Meier. *Taking Control*. Grand Rapids, MI: Baker Book House, 1988.

O'Neill, John, and Pat O'Neill. *Help to Get Help*. Austin, TX: Creative Assistance Press, 1989.

Rogers, Ronald L., and Chandler Scott McMillin. *Freeing Someone You Love from Alcohol and Other Drugs*. Los Angeles: Price Stern Sloan, Inc., 1989.

Rosellini, Gayle, and Mark Worden. *Of Course You Are Angry*. San Francisco: Harper and Row Publishers, Inc., 1986.

Storti, Ed, and Janet Keller. *Crisis Intervention: Acting Against Addiction*. New York: Crown Publishers, Inc., 1988.

VanVonderen, Jeffrey. *Good News for the Chemically Dependent*. Nashville: Thomas Nelson Publishers, 1985.

Chapter 5
Rejecting the Supermom Syndrome

Grollman, Earl A., and Gerri L. Sweder. *The Working Parent Dilemma*. Boston: Beacon Press, 1986.

Groneman, Carol, and Mary Beth Norton. *"To Toil the Livelong Day": American Women at Work, 1780-1980*. Ithaca, NY: Cornell University Press, 1987.

Moore, Louis, and Kay Moore. *When You Both Go to Work*. Waco, TX: Word Books, 1982.

Moster, Mary Beth. *When Mom Goes to Work*. Chicago: Moody Press, 1980.

Chapter 6
Caught in the Middle

Cole, W. Douglas. *When Families Hurt*. Nashville: Broadman Press, 1979.

Dychtwald, Ken. *Age Wave: The Challenges and Opportunities of an Aging America*. Los Angeles: Jeremy P. Tarcher, Inc., 1989.

Foner, Anne. *Aging and Old Age: A New Perspective*. Englewood Cliffs, NJ: Prentice-Hall, Inc., 1986.

Gelfand, Donald E. *The Aging Network*. New York: Springer Publishing Company, Inc., 1988.

Gillies, John. *Care Giving: When Someone You Love Grows Old*. Wheaton, IL.: Harold Shaw Publishers, 1988.

_____. *A Guide to Compassionate Care of the Aging*. Nashville: Thomas Nelson Publishers, 1985.

Manning, Doug. *The Nursing Home Dilemma: How to Make One of Love's Toughest Decisions*. San Francisco: Harper and Row Publishers, Inc., 1986.

McIndoo, Ethel. *Too Late to Say Good-bye*. Birmingham, AL: New Hope, 1988.

MacLean, Helene. *Caring for Your Parents*. Garden City, NY: Doubleday and Company, Inc., 1987.

Portnow, Jay, and Martha Houtmann. *Home Care for the Elderly*. New York: Pocket Books, Inc., 1987.

Rushford, Patricia H. *The Help, Hope and Cope Book for People with Aging Parents*. Old Tappan, NJ.: Fleming II. Revell Company, 1985.

Sommers, Tish, and Laurie Shields. *Women Take Care: The Consequences of Caregiving in Today's Society*. Gainesville, FL: Triad Publishing Company, 1987.

Tournier, Paul. *Learn to Grow Old*. San Francisco: Harper Religious Books, 1983.

Chapter 7
Combating Violence

Family Secrets. Birmingham, AL: New Hope, 1988.

Green, Holly W. *Turning Fear to Hope*. Grand Rapids, MI: Zondervan Publishing House, 1989.

Monfalcone, Wesley R. *Coping with Abuse in the Family*. Philadelphia: Westminster Press, 1980.

NiCarthy, Ginny. *Getting Free*. Seattle, WA: Seal Press, 1986.

NiCarthy, Ginny, Karen Merriam, and Sandra Coffman. *Talking It Out*. Seattle, WA: Seal Press, 1984.

NiCarthy, Ginny, and Sue Davidson. *You Can Be Free*. Seattle, WA: Seal Press, 1989.

Olson, Esther Lee. *No Place to Hide*. Wheaton, IL: Tyndale House Publishers, 1982.

Strom, Kay Marshall. *In the Name of Submission*. Portland, OR: Multnomah Press, 1986.

Walker, Lenore. *The Battered Woman*. New York: Harper and Row Publishers, Inc., 1977.

Chapter 8
The Suicide Threat

Blackburn, Bill. *What You Should Know About Suicide*. Waco, TX: Word Books, 1982.

Cole, W. Douglas. *When Families Hurt*. Nashville: Broadman Press, 1979.

Horton, Marilee. *Dear Mamma, Please Don't Die*. Nashville: Thomas Nelson Publishers, 1979.

Johnston, Jerry. *Why Suicide?* Nashville: Oliver Nelson, 1987.

Klagsbrun, Francine. *Too Young to Die: Youth and Suicide*. New York: Pocket Books, Inc., 1984.

Langford, Mary. *That Nothing Be Wasted*. Birmingham, AL: New Hope, 1988.

Minirth, Frank B., and Paul D. Meier. *Happiness Is a Choice: Overcoming Depression*. Grand Rapids, MI: Baker Book House, 1978.

Yancey, Philip. *Where Is God When It Hurts*. Grand Rapids, MI: Zondervan Publishing House, 1977.

Chapter 9
Counting the Cost

Ferrell, Frank, and Janet Ferrell. *Trevor's Place*. San Francisco: Harper and Row Publishers, Inc., 1985.

Kozol, Jonathan. *Rachel and Her Children: Homeless Families in America.* New York: Ballantine Books, 1988.

Redburn, F. Stevens, and Terry F. Buss. *Responding to America's Homeless*. New York: Praeger Publishers, 1986.

Resener, Carl R. *Crisis in the Streets*. Nashville: Broadman Press, 1988.

Chapter 10
Courage to Care

Hendee, John. *Recruiting, Training, and Developing Volunteer Adult Workers*. Cincinnati: Standard Publishing Company, 1988.

Maves, Paul B. *Older Volunteers in Church and Community: A Manual for Ministry*. Valley Forge, PA: Judson Press, 1981.

McDonough, Reginald M. *Keys to Effective Motivation*. Nashville: Broadman Press, 1979.

——————. *Working with Volunteer Leaders in the Church*. Nashville: Broadman Press, 1976.

O'Connell, Brian. *Effective Leadership in Voluntary Organizations*. Chicago: Association Press, 1976.

Wilson, Marlene. *How to Mobilize Church Volunteers*. Minneapolis, MN: Augsburg Publishing House, 1983.

Bibliography

Alsdurf, James, and Phyllis Alsdurf. "Battered into Submission." *Christianity Today* 33 (June 16, 1989): 24.

Ashker, Helen. *Jesus Cares for Women*. Colorado Springs, CO: NavPress, 1987.

Bloom, David E. "Women and Work." *American Demographics* (September 1986): 26.

Family Violence—The Battered Woman. Austin, TX: League of Women Voters of Texas Education Fund, 1984.

Kelly, Marilynn, ed. "RD Digest," vol. 8, no. 8 (September 1986): 4.

Mason, Diane. "Superwoman's Fall from Role Model to Syndrome." *St. Petersburg Times*, February 16, 1986. Reprinted from *Women*, vol. 3 (Boca Raton, FL: Social Issues Resources Series, 1989): Article no. 43.

McDonough, Reginald M. *Working with Volunteer Leaders in the Church*. Nashville: Broadman Press, 1976.

Nellis, Muriel. *The Female Fix*. Boston: Houghton Mifflin Company, 1980. Reprint. New York: Penguin Books, 1981.

O'Neill, John, and Pat O'Neill. *Help to Get Help*. Austin, TX: Creative Assistance Press, 1989.

Porter, Fran. *Family Violence* Conference Outline. Birmingham, AL: Woman's Missionary Union.

Ray, Barbara R., and Monique C. Braude, eds. *Women and Drugs: A New Era of Research*. Research Monograph 65. Rockville, MD: National Institute on Drug Abuse, 1986.

Sandroff, Ronni. "Caught in the Middle: Caring for Your Aging Parents and Your Children." *Health Report*. Knoxville: Whittle Communications L.P., 1989.

Sledge, Sharlande. "Profile: Frances Booth Porter." *Folio* 7 (Autumn 1989): 4.

Spradlin, Marsha. *LIVINGtouch*. Birmingham, AL: New Hope, 1988.

Strom, Kay Marshall. *Helping Women in Crisis*. Grand Rapids, MI: Ministry Resources Library, 1986.

Tharp, Cliff, comp. "Research Information Report," series 4, no. 13. Nashville: Baptist Sunday School Board, August 1989.

"The Unhealthy Homeless." *The Futurist* (July-August 1989): 56-57.